Win, Lose, or Draw

4th Edition

Dr. Karen Holmes
Butler University

www.kendallhunt.com
Send all inquiries to:
4050 Westmark Drive
Dubuque, IA 52004-1840

Copyright © 2013, 2014, 2016, 2018 by Kendall Hunt Publishing Company

ISBN: 978-1-5249-4995-2

Published in the United States of America

TABLE OF CONTENTS
Win, Lose, or Draw
4th Edition

TEST 1

Logic, Sets, and Combinatorics

GROUP #1

 **The Games We Play**

1.1) In your group, list as many reasons as you can think of why people play games.

1.2) In your group, list all of the different types of games you can (i.e. board games, etc) and list one example of each.

1.3) List three of your favorite games:

    a) played as a child   b) play now

        1)   1)

        2)   2)

        3)   3)

1.4) Go to the internet and look up the history of one of those games from both a) and b) above. Take some notes below about when they were created, by whom, and 2 other interesting facts about each game.

    a) game:

        when created:

        who created it:

        other interesting facts: 1.

                           2.

    b) game:

        when created:

        who created it:

        other interesting facts: 1.

                           2.

GROUP #2

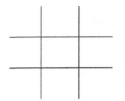 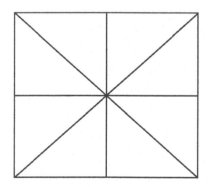

**Paper
Games**

2.1) The origin of Tic Tac Toe is not known precisely, but some say it was played in Egypt as early as 1300 BC. In modern history it was actually the first computer game in the world. Play enough games of Tic Tac Toe with the people in your group to fill in everyone's boards. While playing the games, write down any strategies you found to win or, at least, avoid losing.

corner	side	corner
side	center	side
corner	side	corner

2.2) Another three-in-a-row game from Zimbabwe is called *Tsoro Yemtatu* (*tatu* means "three"). On the diagram below, note that there are 7 intersection points; the object of the game is to get three of your "stones" in a row of intersection points. Each player has three stones which are laid in turn on an intersection point not already occupied. After all stones are laid down, there will be only one open point. The players take turns moving any of their stones to the open point. Whoever gets three in a row wins.

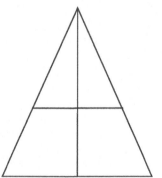 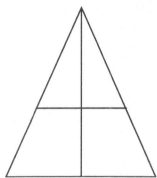

Write any ideas or strategies of how to succeed in winning or avoid losing.

2.3) Another three in a row game played by Asante schoolchildren in southern Ghana is played on a square network marked on the ground. Each player has four sticks or colored stones. Each player in turn places their stones on an intersection point. Once all are placed **players may move one of their markers to an adjacent point**. The object is to place three in a row.

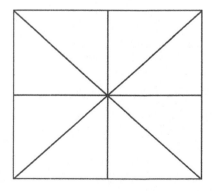

Write any ideas or strategies of how to succeed or avoid losing.

4

2.4) If you've ever played the game Mastermind, **BULLS AND COWS** is the paper and pencil version and has been around for about a century. It is a game played with 2 players (or possibly teams). Here are the general rules:

BULLS AND COWS RULES

1) *Player 1 writes a 3-6 digit secret code where all of the digits are unique (i.e. no repeating digits, like 300).*
2) *Player 2 makes a guess.*
3) *Player 1 will say how many bulls and cows the guess contains.*

> **BULL = a correct digit in the right position**

> **COW = a correct digit in the wrong position**

4) *Player 2 keeps making guesses until they figure out the secret code.*

Example Game:

Player 1's Secret Code: 427
Player 2's Guess #1: 123   Player 1 would say: 1 Bull (for the 2) and 0 Cows
Player 2's Guess #2: 456   Player 1 would say: 1 Bull (for the 4) and 0 Cows
Player 2's Guess #3: 789   Player 1 would say: 0 Bulls and 1 Cow (for the 7)
Player 2's Guess #4: 158   Player 1 would say: 0 Bulls and 0 Cows
Now Player 2 knows 1, 5, 8, and 0 are not in the code, so they would keep guessing....

Play a few games of Bulls and Cows with your group, either breaking into pairs and playing one on one or play two on two. Keep track of how many guesses it takes each of you to get the right code.

a) **Using a 3 digit code:**

      Game 1: code _____ # of guesses _____   Game 2: code _____ # of guesses _____

      Game 3: code _____ # of guesses _____   Game 4: code _____ # of guesses _____

b) Were there any strategies that you used to make you get the code quicker?

c) **Using 4 digit code:**

      Game 1: code _____ # of guesses _____   Game 2: code _____ # of guesses _____

d) What differences did you observe when using a 4 digit code as opposed to a 3 digit code?

e) **Now try a 5 digit code:**

      Game 1: code _____ # of guesses _____   Game 2: code _____ # of guesses _____

2.5) In the game Bulls and Cows, a BULL = correct digit in the right position and a COW = correct digit in the wrong position. Determine the code for each example.

a)

Guess	# of Bulls	# of Cows
1 2 3	1	0
4 5 6	0	1
7 8 9	0	1
1 4 7	1	2

Code: ____ ____ ____

b)

Guess	# of Bulls	# of Cows
1 2 3	0	0
4 5 6	0	3
5 6 4	0	3

Code: ____ ____ ____

c)

Guess	# of Bulls	# of Cows
1 2 3	1	0
4 5 6	0	1
7 8 9	1	0
7 1 4	0	0
3 8 5	0	0

Code: ____ ____ ____

d)

Guess	# of Bulls	# of Cows
1 2 3	0	1
4 5 6	1	0
7 8 9	0	0
2 0 6	1	0

Code: ____ ____ ____

e)

Guess	# of Bulls	# of Cows
1 2 3	0	1
4 5 6	1	0
7 8 9	0	0
4 1 0	0	1
2 0 6	0	2

Code: ____ ____ ____

f)

Guess	# of Bulls	# of Cows
1 2 3	0	1
4 5 6	0	1
7 8 9	0	1
2 4 8	0	1
2 4 7	0	0
8 3 5	1	0

Code: ____ ____ ____

g)

Guess	# of Bulls	# of Cows
1 2 3	1	1
4 5 6	0	0
7 8 9	0	1
7 2 1	0	1
8 1 3	1	0

Code: ____ ____ ____

h)

Guess	# of Bulls	# of Cows
1 2 3	0	1
4 5 6	1	0
7 8 9	0	1
1 6 7	0	0
4 2 8	1	0

Code: ____ ____ ____

6

GRE / LSAT Practice

If you plan on going to grad school or law school, you will probably be asked to take the GRE (Graduate Record Exam) or LSAT (Law School Admission Test). It aims to measure verbal, quantitative, and analytical skills that have developed throughout a person's life. Here are a few of questions similar to some on the GRE or LSAT.

3.1) A nonprofit organization's board of directors, composed of four women (Angela, Betty, Carmine, and Delores) and three men (Ed, Frank, and Grant), holds frequent meetings. A meeting can be held at Betty's house, at Delores's house, or at Frank's house. The following conditions must hold:

Delores cannot attend any meetings at Betty's house.
Carmine cannot attend any meetings on Tuesday or on Friday.
Angela cannot attend any meetings at Delores's house.
Ed can attend only those meetings that Grant also attends.
Frank can attend only those meetings that both Angela and Carmine attend.

a) If all members of the board are to attend a meeting, under which of the following circumstances can it be held?

    i) Monday at Betty's
    ii) Tuesday at Frank's
    iii) Wednesday at Delores's
    iv) Thursday at Frank's
    v) Friday at Betty's

b) Which of the following can be the group that attends a meeting on Wednesday at Betty's?

    i) Angela, Betty, Carmine, Ed, and Frank
    ii) Angela, Betty, Ed, Frank, and Grant
    iii) Angela, Betty, Carmine, Delores, and Ed
    iv) Angela, Betty, Delores, Frank, and Grant
    v) Angela, Betty, Carmine, Frank and Grant

c) If Carmine and Angela attend a meeting but Grant is unable to attend, which of the following could be true?
    The meeting is: i) on Tuesday
                    ii) on Friday
                    iii) at Delores's
    iv) at Frank's
    v) attended by six board members

d) If the meeting is held on Tuesday at Betty's, which of the following pairs can be among the members who attend?

    i) Angela and Frank
    ii) Carmine and Ed
    iii) Carmine and Angela
    iv) Ed and Betty
    v) Frank and Delores

e) If Frank attends a meeting on Thursday that is not held at his house, which of the following must be true?

    i) The group can include, at most, two women.
    ii) The meeting is at Betty's house.
    iii) Ed is not at the meeting.
    iv) Grant is not at the meeting.
    v) Delores is at the meeting.

f) If Grant is unable to attend a meeting on Tuesday at Delores's, what is the largest possible number of members who can attend?

g) If a meeting is held on Friday, list the board member(s) who cannot attend.

3.2) An amusement park roller coaster includes five cars, numbered 1 through 5 from front to back. Each car accommodates up to two riders, seated side by side. Six people—Tom, Gwen, Laurie, Mark, Paul and Jack—are riding the coaster at the same time.

Laurie is sharing a car.
Mark is not sharing a car and is seated immediately behind an empty car.
Tom is not sharing a car with either Gwen or Paul.
Gwen is riding in either the third or fourth car.

a) Which of the following groups of riders could occupy the second car?
        (A) Laurie only   (D) Jack and Tom
        (B) Tom and Gwen   (E) Jack, Gwen, and Paul
        (C) Laurie and Mark

b) If Gwen is riding right behind Laurie's car and right ahead of Tom's car, all of the following must be true EXCEPT:
        (A) Gwen is riding in the fourth car.   (D) Laurie is riding in the third car.
        (B) Paul is riding in the third car.   (E) The first car is empty.
        (C) Tom is riding in the fifth car.

c) Which one of the following statements CANNOT be true?

        (A) Neither Tom nor Gwen is sharing a car with another rider.
        (B) Neither Mark nor Jack is sharing a car with another rider.
        (C) Tom is sharing a car, and Jack is sharing a car.
        (D) Gwen is sharing a car, and Paul is sharing a car.
        (E) Tom is sharing a car, and Gwen is sharing a car.

d) If Paul is riding in the second car, how many different combinations of riders are possible for the third car?

        (A) one   (B) two   (C) three   (D) four   (E) five

e) Assume that a seventh rider is riding with Jack in the first car, but that all other rules remain unchanged. Which of the following is a complete and accurate list of the riders who might be riding in the fifth car?

        (A) Mark   (D) Tom, Laurie, Mark
        (B) Gwen, Paul   (E) Mark, Gwen, Paul, Tom, Laurie
        (C) Tom, Laurie, Paul

3.3) A baseball league has six teams: A, B, C, D, E, and F. All games are played at 7:30pm on Fridays, and there are sufficient fields for each team to play a game every Friday night. Each team must play each other team exactly once, and the following conditions must be met:
                  Team A plays team D first and team F second.
                  Team B plays team E first and team C third.

  a) What is the total number of games that each team must play during the season?

  b) What team must team B play second?

  c) The last set of games could be between which teams?
        i) A and B; C and F; D and E   iv) A and D; B and C; E and F
        ii) A and B; C and D; E and F   v) A and D; B and E; C and F
        iii) A and C; B and E; D and F

  d) If team D wins five games, which of the following must be true?
        i) Team A loses five games.   iv) Team B wins five games.
        ii) Team A wins four games.   v) Team B loses at least one game.
        iii) Team A wins its first game.

3.4) In an executive parking lot, there are six parking spaces in a row; labeled 1 through 6. Exactly five cars of 5 different colors- black, gray, pink, white, and yellow- are to be parked in the spaces. The cars can park in any of the spaces as long as the following conditions are met:

The pink car must be parked in space 3.
The black car must be parked in a space next to the space in which the yellow car is parked.
The gray car cannot be parked in a space next to the space in which the white car is parked.

a) If the yellow car is parked in space 1, how many acceptable parking arrangements are there for the five cars?

b) Which of the following must be true of any acceptable parking arrangement?

    i) One of the cars is parked in space 2.
    ii) One of the cars is parked in space 6.
    iii) There is an empty space next to the space in which the yellow car is parked.
    iv) There is an empty space next to the space in which the gray car is parked.
    v) Either the black car or the yellow car is parked in a space next to space 3.

c) If the gray car is parked in space 2, none of the cars can be parked in which space?

d) What spaces can the white car not park in?

3.5) Two collectors, John and Jack, are each selecting a group of three posters from a group of seven movie posters: J, K, L, M, N, O, and P. No poster can be in both groups. The selections made by John and Jack are subject to the following restrictions:

If K is in John's group, M must be in Jack's group.
If N is in John's group, P must be in Jack's group.
J and P cannot be in the same group.
M and O cannot be in the same group.

a) Which of the following pairs of groups selected by John and Jack conform to the restrictions?
    i) John: J, K, L   Jack: M, N, O
    ii)   J, K, P   L, M, N
    iii)   K, N, P   J, M, O
    iv)   L, M, N   K, O, P
    v)   M, O, P   J, K, N

b) If N is in John's group, which poster(s) could not be in Jack's group?

c) If K and N are in John's group, what three posters must be in Jack's group?

d) If J is in Jack's group, which of the following is true?
    i) K cannot be in John's group   iv) P must be John's group
    ii) N cannot be in John's group   v) P must be in Jack's group
    iii) O cannot be in Jack's group

e) If K is in John's group, which of the following is true?
    i) J must be in John's group   iv) N cannot be in John's group
    ii) O must be in John's group   v) O cannot be in Jack's group
    iii) L must be in Jack's group

3.6) An athlete has six trophies to place on an empty three-shelf display case. The six trophies are bowling trophies F, G, and H and tennis trophies J, K, and L. The three shelves of the display case are labeled 1 to 3 from top to bottom. Any of the shelves can remain empty and hold any number of trophies. The athlete's placement of the trophies must conform to the following conditions:

- J and L cannot be of the same shelf.
- F must be on the shelf immediately above the shelf that L is on.
- No single shelf can hold all three bowling trophies.
- K cannot be on Shelf 2.

a) If G and H are on Shelf 2, which of the following must be true?

    A) K is on Shelf 1.   D) G and J are on the same shelf.
    B) L is on Shelf 2.   E) F and K are on the same shelf.
    C) J is on Shelf 3.

b) If no tennis trophies are on Shelf 3, which pair of trophies must be on the same shelf?

    A) F and G   D) K and J
    B) L and H   E) G and H
    C) L and G

c) If J is on Shelf 2, which of the following must also be on Shelf 2?

    A) K   D) L
    B) G   E) H
    C) F

d) If Shelf 1 remains empty, which of the following must be FALSE?

    A) H and F are on the same shelf.
    B) There are exactly three trophies on Shelf 2.
    C) G and H are on the same shelf.
    D) There are exactly two trophies on Shelf 3.
    E) G and K are on the same shelf.

e) If L and G are on the same shelf, and if one of the shelves remains empty, which of the following must be true?

    A) If H is on Shelf 3, then J is on Shelf 2.
    B) K and L are on the same shelf.
    C) If H is on Shelf 2, then J is on Shelf 3.
    D) F and K are on the same shelf.
    E) If J is on Shelf 2, then H is on Shelf 1.

3.7) After the goalie has been chosen, the Smalltown Bluebirds hockey team has a starting lineup that is selected from 2 groups. 1st Group: **John, Dexter, Bart, Erwin** and 2nd Group: **Leanne, Roger, George, Marlene, Patricia**. When deciding on the players in the lineup, the coach considers the following requirements:

    George will only start if Bart also starts.
    Dexter and Bart will not start together.
    If George starts, Marlene won't start.
    The 4 fastest players are: John, Bart, George and Patricia
    3 of the 4 fastest players will always be chosen.
    Two players are always chosen from the first group, while three are chosen from the second group.

a) If Marlene is in the starting lineup, which of the players will be the first group players who will also be starting?

    A. Erwin and Dexter   C. John and Bart   E. Erwin and Bart
    B. John and Dexter   D. Dexter and Bart

b) Of the following hockey players, who must start?

    A. Patricia   C. George   E. Marlene
    B. John   D. Bart

GROUP #4

Logic Puzzles

4.1) Five people are tennis players. From the clues below, work out the club where each plays (**Worthies, Servers, Nets, Matches, Racquets**), what their surname is (**Atkins, Evans, Harrison, Kelly, Brown**), and how old they are (**18, 30, 43, 55, 61**)?

1. Margaret joined Worthies club last summer, and hopes to still be playing when she hits 40.
2. Stephen isn't at Servers, whose member is the second oldest and isn't a Kelly.
3. Anne, the youngest player, isn't a Harrison, and doesn't play at Nets, the club of Mr. Brown.
4. Racquets only has male members - Carlos would never join it and Margaret Kelly can't!
5. Clive is the second eldest player, being junior to Stephen Atkins.

First Name	Anne	Carlos	Clive	Margaret	Stephen
Surname					
Club					
Age					

4.2) In horse racing, there are three races that make up the Triple Crown: the Kentucky Derby, the Preakness, and the Belmont. All three races have only been won by the same horse nine times in over 100 years of events. Let's say there are four popular horses signed up to run in the Kentucky Derby (**Galloping Grocer, Alec's Pride, OneForTheMoney, EatMyDust**). While all four of them placed in the top four winners, none of them placed in the same position as their starting post position (the gate number where each horse started the race from: either **2, 5, 6, 7**). Determine the name of each racehorse, their starting post positions, the winning placement of each horse, and the stable colors of each racehorse (**Green and Black, Hot Pink, Blue and White, Purple and White**).

1. Galloping Grocer didn't have hot pink stable colors.
2. The fourth place horse didn't have the post position 2.
3. The second place horse had a larger numbered post position than OneForTheMoney, but a smaller post position than Galloping Grocer.
4. Eat My Dust had a post position one larger than the horse with blue & white stable colors.
5. The purple and white stable colors belonged to the horse who won third place.
6. The horse with post position 7 won the race.
7. Alec's Pride had the green & black stable colors.
8. The horse at post position 5 was not OneForTheMoney.

Place	1st	2nd	3rd	4th
Name				
Post Position				
Stable Colors				

4.3) CLUE: Four friends: Bob, Sue, Allen, and Erin, played a very intense game of Clue. A weapon, suspect, and room card were secretly chosen and the rest of the cards were handed out. Bob and Sue each had 5 cards in their hand while Allen and Erin each only had 4. Based on the following information, figure out who had what cards and from that determine who killed Mr. Boddy, with what weapon, and in what room? **(No one bluffs unless it's specifically noted.)**

Mark √ = don't have the card
■ = have the card

SUSPECTS	B	S	A	E
Colonel Mustard				
Professor Plum				
Mr. Green				
Mrs. Peacock				
Miss Scarlett				
Mrs. White				
WEAPONS				
Knife				
Candlestick				
Revolver				
Rope				
Lead Pipe				
Wrench				
ROOMS				
Hall				
Lounge				
Dining Room				
Kitchen				
Ballroom				
Conservatory				
Billiard Room				
Library				
Study				

- Neither Erin nor Sue had Miss Scarlet.

- Bob asked Allen if he had Mrs. Peacock, Revolver, and Hall, but Allen had none of these cards.

- Erin asked Allen if he had Prof Plum, Lead Pipe, and Dining Room; Allen had one of these which he showed her.

- Bob had more than one weapon, while Allen just had one.

- Sue asked Erin if she had Mrs. Peacock, Knife, and Billiard Room. Erin has 2 of these and showed Sue the weapon.

- Allen dropped the Lounge card, which was his only room, on the floor and all the other players saw it.

- Erin was upset that she did not get Mrs. Peacock, her favorite character.

- Bob accidentally showed Allen the Conservatory even though that was not one Allen requested.

- Sue always thought that if she were to murder someone it would be with a Revolver, so she was pleased that she had the card.

- Erin asked Bob is he had the Library, Rope, and Prof Plum. Bob was only able to show the suspect.

- Allen is starting to think that it was Mr. Green with the Wrench in the Conservatory. However, Allen is very bad at Clue and none of his guesses were right (especially since he has Mr. Green's card!).

- Erin is starving and is reminded of this every time she looks at her Kitchen card, one of her three room cards.

- Sue has two suspect cards.

- Allen is very confused about how one would use the Lead Pipe to kill someone. He thinks that you would use it to give them lead poisoning. He has that card.

- Sue wonders why there is a room that is the Hall (she has the card). Wouldn't all the space between the rooms be the hall?

- Allen asked Bob if he had Mrs. White, Rope, and Ballroom. Bob lies and says that he has none of them even though he does possess the Ballroom but none of the others.

- Bob is pleased that he has the Candlestick card because he has an affinity for shiny objects. He also has the Wrench, but his feelings for that card are not the same.

- Sue was reminded by her Dining Room card that she was 45 minutes late for the party she was hosting, and had to leave, thus ending the game without any of them knowing who did it....

Suspect: _____   Weapon: _____   Room:_____

4.4) THE PRICE IS RIGHT There are 5 contestants on The Price is Right, **Bob, Betty, Sue, Tom**, and **Lindsay**. Each of the contestants played a different game from the following games: *Now and Then* (pricing grocery items), *Cliff Hangers* (you "climb" a mountain), *Plinko* (drop discs down a board to land in different slots at the bottom), *Master Key* (open a lock with a key), and *Dice Game* (roll large dice to win a car). The contestants' ages are **20, 30, 40, 50**, or **60** and they won **nothing, a bedroom set, a car, a trip to the Bahamas**, or **$10,000**. Use the following clues to fill in the grid.

- It's Bob's 60th birthday today.
- Betty thought that shaving cream cost $3.29 now, but the real price was $2.67 so she lost her game.
- Sue loves rock climbing so her game fit her perfectly.
- Lindsay won 5 discs for her game by really only needed 1 since she landed on the $10,000 on her first drop.
- Betty is the youngest contestant.
- Tom rolled a 2 and thought that his prize was higher than what he rolled. He was right and won!
- Lindsay is halfway to Bob's age.
- Sue did not win the bedroom set.
- Tom is the second oldest contestant.

Name	Game	Winnings	Age
Bob			
Betty			
Sue			
Tom			
Lindsay			

4.5) Bill is a contestant on *Deal or No Deal*. There are 10 cases (labeled 1-10) with hidden cash values of $0.01, $1, $10, $20, $100, $500, $1000, $2500, $5000, and $10,000. The first case Bill picks will not be opened until the end and the others are opened as soon as they're picked to reveal the prize he doesn't win. Determine the order that Bill **picked** the cases using the following hints.

- Bill picked an odd numbered case first which won't be opened until the end.
- Bill was worried when his second choice case revealed $5000.
- Case #6, which was opened immediately after case #10, had $1000.
- When Bill picked his 5th case and then opened it, he realized that he should have picked Case #3 at the start.
- Case #5 had the lowest value and was picked last.
- Case #10 was opened two turns after the $10,000 prize.
- Bill didn't start with Case #1 or 7.
- Case #8 was picked 9th.
- After Bill was disappointed that he found the $10,000, he opened Case #1 to find Benjamin Franklin inside.
- Case #7 was opened before Case #2 and has 1/10 of the value of Case #4 which was picked 2nd.
- The case that was picked 7th has the same value as its case number.
- Bill kept his original case until the end. When it was opened, he was happy that its value was one of the top three prizes.
- Case #2 has a higher value than Case #8.

order	1st	2nd	3rd	4th	5th	6th	7th	8th	9th	10th
prize										
case #										

13

4.6) MINUTE TO WIN IT is a game show on which contestants have to try to do challenge in less than one minute. The challenges use common household objects and you work up to possibly winning $1 million. Tommy was a contestant on Minute To Win It and he ended up being extremely good at the game and won $1 million! Using the clues below, determine the following elements:

- what challenges he did: **Balance the Bulb, Bobblehead, Movin' On Up, Back Flip, Uphill Battle, Keep It Up, Sticky Situation, Egg Tower, Bottoms Up**
- what level the challenges were (their order): **1, 2, 3, 4, 5, 6, 7, 8, 9**
- his winning time for each challenge: **27, 32, 39, 41, 43, 46, 52, 58, 60**
- what household item he used for the challenge: **Pedometer, Yo-Yo, Cups, Bread, Marbles, Pencils, Feathers, Paper Towel, Salt**

1. The 1st challenge wasn't his fastest time.
2. The challenge that used Pencils was definitely not the fastest time either but was faster than the Bottoms Up challenge.
3. The challenge that took the longest required using marbles.
4. Movin' On Up, Bobblehead, and the 4th challenge all took less than 40 seconds.
5. Tommy was familiar with Pedometers which made the second challenge the fastest.
6. Tommy got his 4th fastest time doing the Keep It Up challenge.
7. Back Flip was the second to last challenge right after Bottoms Up and right before the challenge that used Marbles.
8. Uphill Battle did not use Paper Towels.
9. It was really hard for Tommy to Balance the Bulb on Salt in the 4th challenge.
10. The Cups challenge which was his 1st challenge was done in 32 seconds.
11. Pencils were not part of the Keep It Up challenge but were used in the challenge that took 52 seconds.
12. Sticky Situation was difficult and took more time than Keep It Up but less than Back Flip.
13. Movin' On Up took more than 30 seconds.
14. The 6th challenge used Feathers and took 41 seconds.
15. Sticky Situation took over 45 seconds but was faster than the challenge that took 52 seconds.
16. The 3rd challenge used Bread and took 46 seconds.
17. Bottoms Up took the second longest times and did not use Paper Towels.

level	1	2	3	4	5	6	7	8	9
challenge									
time									
object									

GROUP #5

More
Logic Puzzles

In this project, your group is going to try writing your own logic puzzle. It can be short and sweet; just make sure you have at least 3 choices for each of 3 categories. To write your own logic puzzle, it seems best to start with your solution and go backwards to give clues. When you're done, you will be switching with another group so make sure you have a legible copy at the end.

5.1) **MONOPOLY** **Aaden, Rachel, Karen, Colin, Laura, Scott, Joel,** and **Billy** are playing a leisurely afternoon game of Monopoly. They each have a different piece to play with, a **wheelbarrow**, a **thimble**, a **ship**, a **cannon**, a **moneybag**, a **racecar**, a **dog**, and an **iron**. Figure out what piece each player has and where that piece is located on the board.

Top row:

| Free Parking | RED Kentucky ($220) | Chance | RED Indiana ($220) | RED Illinois ($240) | B & O Railroad ($200) | YELLOW Atlantic ($260) | YELLOW Ventnor ($260) | Water Works ($150) | YELLOW Marvin Gardens ($280) | Go To Jail |

Left column (top to bottom): ORANGE New York ($200); ORANGE Tennessee ($180); Community Chest; ORANGE St. James ($180); Pennsylvania RR ($200); MAGENTA Virginia ($160); MAGENTA State ($140); Electric Company ($150); MAGENTA St. Charles ($140)

Right column (top to bottom): GREEN Pacific ($300); GREEN North Carolina ($300); Community Chest; GREEN Pennsylvania ($320); Shortline RR ($200); Chance; DARK BLUE Park Place ($350); Luxury Tax; DARK BLUE Boardwalk ($400)

Bottom row:

| JAIL | LT BLUE Conneticut ($120) | LT BLUE Vermont ($100) | Chance | LT BLUE Oriental ($100) | Reading Railroad ($200) | Income Tax | PURPLE Baltic ($60) | Community Chest | PURPLE Mediterranean ($60) | GO (collect $200) |

Clues:

One piece is on a railroad.
The cannon is directly next to the Luxury Tax space.
Park Place and Mediterranean Ave are not occupied.
Colin has the piece that starts with the same letter as his first name.
Billy's piece is related to his love for cash.
Karen bought her property for $320.
Laura just missed her favorite utility but has yet to avoid a confrontation with a police officer.
Scott's piece must have caused him to speed and was punished.
A girl's piece is not located on a railroad.
Billy's piece is between Rachel and Laura's piece.
Karen loves the color green and her purchase reflects this.
The ship and the cannon are on the same row, opposite to the wheelbarrow.
Despite his dislike of gardening, Joel picked his piece last and ends up with a gardening tool.
Laura's piece is related to her love for animals.
The railroad where the piece is located is in the same row as Water Works.
The person with the thimble is directly next to the free parking space.
The thimble and the dog are on the same row as the moneybag.
Joel's property is more than $130 and less than $150.
No two piece are next to each other.
None of the orange spaces are occupied.
A girl has the ship piece.
Aaden only has $60 to buy a property.

PIECE   LOCATION

Aaden _____ _____

Rachel _____ _____

Karen _____ _____

Colin _____ _____

Laura _____ _____

Scott _____ _____

Joel _____ _____

Billy _____ _____

16

5.2) Eight heavyweight-boxing champions (**Sultan, Mike, George, Muhammad, Ingemar, Max, Jess,** and **James**) of different years (**1892, 1915, 1930, 1959, 1978, 1994, 1996,** and **2007**) have recently decided to hold a tournament to see who is the Ultimate Heavyweight Champion of the World. Before they held the competition, they wanted to see what their chances of winning were based on how many matches they've competed in (**24, 25, 28, 35, 58, 61, 70,** and **81**) and how many matches they've won (**16, 22, 26, 26, 50, 56, 56,** and **76**). From the clues below, figure out each competitor's last name (**Johansson, Foreman, Ibragimov, Willard, Corbett, Ali, Schmeling,** and **Tyson**), their first name, the number of matches in total they've competed in, and the number of matches they've won.

Muhammad and Max have both won the same number of matches. So have Johansson and Willard.

In 1892, the champion won 16 matches. In 1930, the champion competed in 70 matches.

Muhammad Ali was named the heavy-weight champ in 1978 and won 56 matches.

Tyson won in the early 90's and had a penchant for ears.

Mike won 50 matches 35 years after Foreman who won 76.

Sultan's last name and Johansson's first name begin with an "I".

James was the first to win out of the group and Ingemar was the most recent.

Max's last name is not Willard, but a man whose first name starts with a "J" does have that last name.

The champ with the last name identical to a meat company has the first name of Mike and he has competed in 33 more matches than the first competitor.

The man with the last name of Foreman and the most number of matches competed in is the same man who sells miniature grills.

The man with the initials J.W. comes directly in between James and Max, and has won 26 matches. He has also competed in 10 more matches than Corbett.

James Corbett competed in 25 matches.

Sultan has competed in 1 less match than Corbett.

Ingemar has competed in an even number of matches.

year	1892	1915	1930	1959	1978	1994	1996	2007
first name								
last name								
# matches								
# wins								

GROUP #6

1	2	4	3
3	4	1	2
4	3	2	1
2	1	3	4

Sudoku Puzzles

	5	9				3	8	
2			9		1			6
8				7				2
9								3
1								5
	2						7	
		1				8		
			5		6			
				2				

A Sudoku puzzle is a game of logic so reasoning skills and concentration are useful to complete one. The rules for a Sudoku are as follows: the digits 1 through the number of rows/columns can only appear once in every row, column and shaded or unshaded box. The clues are the digits already placed in the puzzle. Also remember: **DON'T GUESS!!!**

6.1) In a sudoku puzzle, some of the numbers are given and the goal is to fill in the blank cells. Consider the puzzle below.

1		4	
			1
2		3	
	3		

Here are some hints:

a) There must be a 1 somewhere in the third row, and the only empty cells in the row are in the 2nd and 4th columns. Why can't the 1 go in the 4th column? Fill in the entire third row.

b) Next consider the lower right-hand box, which now needs a 1 and a 2. There is only one choice for the 1 (why?). Fill in the remainder of the grid.

6.2) Fill in the following sudoku puzzles.

a)

1	2		
3	4		
		1	2
		3	4

b)

	2		
			3
1			
		4	

c)

1			
			3
	1		
		4	

d)

			3
	1		
1			
		2	

6.3) Now try 6 by 6 sudoku puzzle.

a)

1			4		
4				3	
6				1	
	5				2
				6	
5					3

b)

		6	2		
4		5		1	6
		1	6		
		2	5		
5	1				2
		4	1		

18

6.4) The most common size of sudoku is a 9 x 9.

One strategy to try is to identify an empty cell and determine which numbers could fill it. For example, the cell in the first column of the second row is empty. The row contains the numbers 2, 3, 4, 5, and 8; the column contains 1, 2, 7, 8 and 9; and the box contains 1, 2, 4, and 5. The only number not in any of the three lists is 6, so that number must go into that cell.

Another strategy is to choose a number missing from a row, column, or box and try to place it correctly. For example, the third row needs a 3 and has blank cells in the 2nd, 4th, and 9th rows. There is already a 3 in columns 2 and 4, so the 9th cell in the third column must be a 3. Continue with these and other strategies you find to fill in the remainder of the puzzle

2				1		6		
	4		3	8			5	2
1		5		4	6	7	9	
9		8		5	2	3	4	
	3		4	6			1	8
	1				3		7	
8	2	4				1	5	
			6	7				
7	6	1			8	4		

6.5) Fill in the 9 x 9 Sudokus.

5		3	8	1	9		2	
8	1		4			3	9	5
	4	2				7	8	1
6		8	3		1		7	
								8
1		9	5	7			4	6
2				8		9	5	3
		5		9	6			
4			7		5	8	6	2

					6	4	1	2
1			2			6		9
	9			8				
			5					8
	6	1	8		7	3	4	
8					2			
				1				
9		3			5			6
7	8	4	3				2	

SETS and VENN DIAGRAMS NOTES

SET: any group or collection of well-defined objects called **elements**, denoted by listing the elements inside **set braces** { }

$\emptyset$ = { } **Empty or Null Set** = the set containing no elements

$\in$ **"is an element of"** ex. $1 \in \{1,2,3\}$

$\notin$ **"is not an element of"** ex. $4 \notin \{1,2,3\}$

= **"is equal to"**; A = B if A and B have exactly the same elements ex. $\{1,2,3\} = \{2,3,1\}$

$\subseteq$ **"is a subset of"**; $A \subseteq B$ if every element in A is in B, subsets always use set braces ex. $\{1,2\} \subseteq \{1,2,3\}$

$\not\subseteq$ **"is not a subset of"** ex. $\{1, 4\} \not\subseteq \{1, 2, 3\}$

Every set A has _____ and _____ as a subset.

Ex1. Fill in the blanks with $\in$, $\notin$, =, $\subseteq$, or $\not\subseteq$.

a) $\emptyset$ _____ {a, b, c}   b) a _____ {a, b, c}   c) {a} _____ {a, b, c}

d) d _____ {a, b, c}   e) {d} _____ {a, b, c}   f) {b, c, a} _____ {a, b, c}

$\cap$ **AND intersection** $A \cap B$ is the set of all elements in both A **and** B, i.e. what's in common

ex. $\{1, 2, 3, 4\} \cap \{2, 4, 5\} =$

$\cup$ **OR union** $A \cup B$ is the set of all elements in either A **or** B **or** both, i.e. both sets together

ex. $\{1, 2, 3, 4\} \cup \{2, 4, 5\} =$

universal set U is the set of elements being considered (the big set)

complement A^c of a set A is the set of elements of the universal set U that are not in A.

ex. If U = {1, 2, 3, 4, 5, 6, 7} and A = {3, 4, 5, 6}, then $A^c =$ _____.

Note: $\emptyset^c =$ _____ and $U^c =$ _____

Ex2. Given D = {2, 4, 6, 8}, E = {1, 3, 5, 7}, F = {1, 2, 3, 4, 9}, and U = {1, 2, 3, 4, 5, 6, 7, 8, 9, 10}, determine

a) D ∩ E = _____

b) E ∩ F = _____

c) D^C = _____

d) E ∪ F = _____

e) D ∪ (E ∩ F) = _____

f) (E ∪ F) ∩ D^C = _____

g) (E ∪ F)^C = _____

h) E^C ∩ F^C = _____

De Morgan's Laws For all sets A and B, (A ∪ B)^C = A^C ∩ B^C and (A ∩ B)^C = A^C ∪ B^C

cardinality of set A n(A) = the number of elements in set A

ex. If A = {a, b, c}, B = ∅, and C = {0}, then n(A) =____, n(B) =____, n(C) =____.

VENN DIAGRAMS are a pictorial way of demonstrating sets. The box as a whole represents all members of the universal set and A and B are sets with

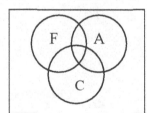

w = in neither A nor B   **x** = in A but not B

y = in B but not A   **z** = in both A and B

Ex3. A survey of college students asked if they play intramural field hockey (F), archery (A), or cricket (C). Shade the areas representing and write in set notation:

a) archery or cricket

b) field hockey and cricket

c) field hockey and cricket but not archery

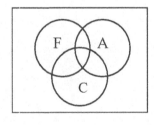

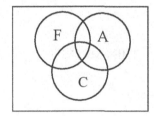

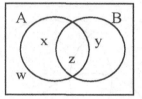

_____

_____

_____

INCLUSION-EXCLUSION PRINCIPLE $n(A \cup B) = n(A) + n(B) - n(A \cap B)$

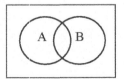 = 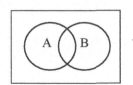 + 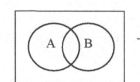 −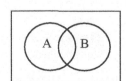

Ex4. If $n(A) = 800$, $n(B) = 200$, $n(A \cup B) = 900$, find $n(A \cap B) =$ _____

Ex5. If 20 students like chemistry, 30 like math, and 10 like both chemistry and math, how many like chemistry or math?

Ex6. 1000 households were asked how they got their sports scores:

740 internet	350 internet and ESPN but not the newspaper
540 ESPN	180 internet and newspaper
280 newspaper	100 ESPN, newspaper, and internet
	60 newspaper, but not internet or ESPN

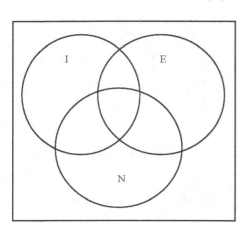

How many got their scores from:

a) internet, but not newspaper or ESPN?   b) ESPN or internet?

c) ESPN or newspaper but not internet?   d) ESPN and newspaper?

THE EMPTY SET

Circle True or False for each statement.

a) $\varnothing \in \varnothing$ T   F   b) $\varnothing \subseteq \{0\}$ T   F

c) $\varnothing = \{0\}$ T   F   d) $\varnothing \subseteq \{\varnothing\}$ T   F

e) $\varnothing = \varnothing$ T   F   f) $\varnothing = \{\varnothing\}$ T   F

g) $\varnothing \subseteq A$ for all sets A   T   F   h) $\varnothing \subseteq \varnothing$ T   F

i) $\varnothing \in \{\varnothing\}$ T   F   j) $\varnothing = 0$ T   F

HOMEWORK PROBLEMS:

1) Given $U = (1,2,3,4,5,6,7,8,9)$, $A = \{2,3,4,5\}$, $B = \{1,7\}$, and $C = \{9\}$, determine the following:

    a) $A \cup B$ b) $A \cap B$ c) A^C

    d) $n(A \cup C)$ e) $(A \cup B)^C \cup C$

    f) $\emptyset \nsubseteq U$ true   false   g) $7 \in B$ true   false   h) $\{7\} \in B$ true   false

2) Given the universal set U = {Al, Bob, Dan, Ed, Jan, Kim, Sue} and the set of those who know how to swim S = {Bob, Ed, Jan, Kim} and the set of those who know how to skateboard B = {Al, Kim, Sue}, find the elements of the indicated sets.

    a) $S \cap B$ b) those who can swim or skateboard   c) B^C

    d) those who cannot swim   e) $S \cup B$ f) those who can skateboard and swim

    g) $S^C \cap B$ h) those who can swim or cannot skateboard

    i) those who can neither swim nor skateboard

3) Given the universal set U = {red, blue, green, orange, yellow, purple, white} and the following race car paints: car X = {red, blue}, car Y = {green, orange, red}, and car Z = {orange, white, red}, determine the indicated sets.

    a) $X \cap Y \cap Z$ b) $(X \cap Y \cap Z)^C$ c) $X \cup (Y \cap Z)$

    d) $X \cup Y \cup Z$ e) $(X \cap Y)^C \cap Z$ f) $(X \cup Y \cup Z)^C$

4) Given the Venn diagram and n(U) =25, determine the following:

a) $n(A \cap B)$ b) $n(A \cup B)$ c) $n(A)$ d) $n(B)$

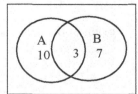

e) $n(A \cap B^C)$ f) $n(A^C \cup B)$ g) $n(A \cap B)^C$ h) $n(A \cup B)^C$

5) A survey of 1500 people in NYC showed that 1140 like the Yankees, 680 like the Mets, and 120 cheer for neither team. Draw a Venn diagram.

      a) How many cheer for both teams?   b) How many cheer only for the Yankees?

6) A group of 32 play bridge every other Tuesday at the senior center (eight tables of four). If 17 of the bridge players like salty snacks, 25 like sweet snacks, and all of the players like at least one of the kinds of snacks; how many like both sweet and salty snacks? Draw a Venn diagram.

7) In a survey of 100 people, 41 reported that they had played Chutes & Ladders when they were young and 65 reported that they played Candyland when they were young, and 25 had played both as youngsters. Draw a Venn diagram to determine the how many people:

      a) played only Candyland?   b) played only Chutes & Ladders?

      c) played neither of these games?   d) did not play Candyland?

      e) played Chutes & Ladders or Candyland?

8) A certain number of students who read the Star newspaper were surveyed. The findings were: 37 will work the crossword puzzle, 32 will work the sudoku, 9 will work both the crossword puzzle and sudoku, and 12 will work neither puzzle. Draw a Venn diagram to determine how many will work:

      a) crossword puzzle or sudoku?   b) only the sudoku?

      c) not work the sudoku?   d) How many were surveyed?

9) Of 80 Carmel High School's varsity athletes, 30 play soccer, 25 play hockey, 40 play football, 6 play soccer and hockey, 8 play hockey and football, 5 play football and soccer but not hockey, and 4 play all three sports. Fill in the Venn diagram to determine the how many athletes:

a) play only soccer?

b) play soccer or hockey?

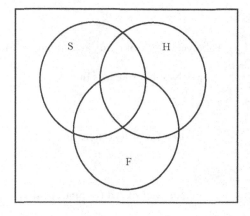

c) play football or hockey?

d) play only one of these sports?

e) play football, hockey, or soccer?

10) An activity director for a cruise ship has surveyed 240 passengers. Of the 240 passengers, 135 like swimming, 150 like dancing, 65 like games, 65 like swimming and dancing but not games, 40 like swimming and games, 25 like dancing and games, and 15 like all three activities. Fill in the Venn diagram and answer how many passengers:

a) like exactly 2 of 3 activities?

b) like only swimming?

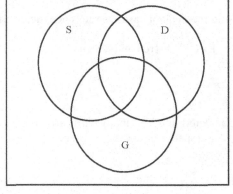

c) like none of these activities?

11) A survey of 770 dentists office indicates that 305 subscribe to Golf magazine, 290 to Field & Stream (FS), 190 to only Sports Illustrated (SI), 110 to Golf and FS, 50 to FS and SI but not Golf, 150 to Golf and SI, and 85 to all three magazines. Fill in the Venn diagram. How many of the surveyed dentist offices subscribe to:

a) exactly one of these magazines?

b) Sports Illustrated?

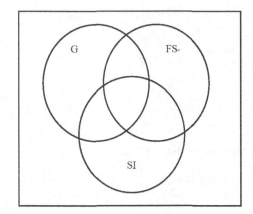

c) Golf or Field & Stream?

d) Sports Illustrated or Field & Stream but not Golf?

GROUP #7

Deck of Cards
and
Set Operations

7.1) Take your deck of cards and organize it in suits from ace, 2, 3, … 10, J, Q, K and determine the following:

a) Number of cards in a deck:

e) List the cards in each suit (also known as **ranks**):

b) List the **suits** (name and symbol) with their color:

f) Number of cards of each rank:

c) Number of red (or black) cards:

g) List the ranks considered face cards:

d) Number of clubs (or any other single suit):

h) Number of face cards:

Using the deck of cards as reference, determine how many cards are contained in the following sets:

Ex1: X = {red and queen} = red ∩ Q

Ex2: Y = {red or queen} = red ∪ Q

$$n(X) = \underline{\qquad}$$

$$n(Y) = \underline{\qquad}$$

7.2) Determine how many cards are in the following sets.

a) A = {spades or aces} = ♠ ∪ ace

b) B = {threes or face} = 3 ∪ 6

$$n(A) = \underline{\qquad}$$

$$n(B) = \underline{\qquad}$$

c) C = {face or black} = face ∪ black

d) D = {clubs and twos} = ♣ ∩ 2

$$n(C) = \underline{\qquad}$$

$$n(D) = \underline{\qquad}$$

e) E = {aces or eights} = aces ∪ 8

f) F = {face and diamonds} = face ∩ ♦

$$n(E) = \underline{\qquad}$$

$$n(F) = \underline{\qquad}$$

g) G = {jacks and face cards} = J ∩ face

h) H = {face and black} = face ∩ black

$$n(G) = \underline{\qquad}$$

$$n(H) = \underline{\qquad}$$

i) I = {queens or face cards} = Q ∪ face

j) J = {aces and eights} = ace ∩ 8

$$n(I) = \underline{\qquad}$$

$$n(J) = \underline{\qquad}$$

k) K = {not hearts nor spades} = $(\heartsuit \cup \spadesuit)^C$ l) L = {spades and not tens} = $\spadesuit \cap 10^C$

n(K) = _____   n(L) = _____

m) M = {sevens or kings, but not clubs} = $(7 \cup K) \cap \clubsuit^C$ n) N = {nines or red, but not kings} = $(9 \cup red) \cap K^C$

n(M) = _____   n(N) = _____

7.3) Now we will investigate how many subsets are possible in a set with a certain number of elements. For each of the given sets, list all possible subsets, starting with the zero element subset, then one element subset(s), and so on.

a) A = {three of spades} = {3$\spadesuit$}   b) B = {jack of diamonds, two of hearts} = {J$\diamond$, 2$\heartsuit$}

c) C = {four of clubs, queen of hearts, ace of spades} = {4$\clubsuit$, Q$\heartsuit$, A$\spadesuit$}

d) D = {five of diamonds, king of clubs, seven of diamonds, 10 of hearts} = {5$\diamond$, K$\clubsuit$, 7$\diamond$, 10$\heartsuit$}

e) Now count your subsets:

of A = _____   of B = _____   of C = _____   of D = _____

f) Make a speculation as to how many subsets a set with **n** elements would have.

7.4) You have some friends over for a friendly poker tournament.

a) You decide to order pizza, but when you call the pizza place says they're out of everything except pepperoni, anchovies, clams, mushrooms, and green peppers. How many different pizzas can you order?

b) You all decide you want more choices, so you call another pizza place. They offer 8 different toppings and advertise that they offer over 250 different pizzas. Are they correct?

c) What is the minimum number of toppings that this pizza place must have available if it wants to offer at least 1000 different types of pizza?

d) If you have invited 6 friends for this tournament, how many different groups could you have show up for your tournament?

7.5) Hoyle (a company that produces playing cards) did a survey of card players. They decided to use the following Venn diagram to help illustrate the results of their survey. S = {those who like to play solitaire}, P = {those who like to play poker}, And B = {those who like to play bridge}. Shade in the regions that represent and describe using set notation:

a) those who like to play poker,
   but not solitaire

b) those who like bridge
   and solitaire

c) those who don't like poker
   and do not like bridge
   (same as those who don't
   like poker or bridge)

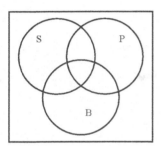

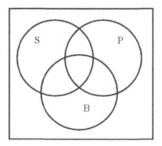

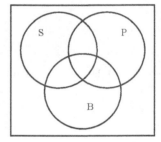

Set notation: _____   _____   _____

d) Using the same sets, S, P, and B, describe the shaded region and then put it in set notation (using unions, intersections, complements, etc).

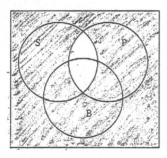

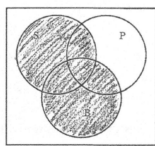

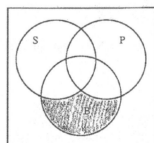

i) describe in words: ii) describe in words: iii) describe in words:

set notation _____   set notation _____   set notation_____

28

7.6) Determine the set notation and the number of cards in each set.

a) A = {fives or face} = _____

   n(A) = _____

b) B = {hearts and face} = _____

   n(B) = _____

c) C = {neither red nor clubs} = _____

   n(C) = _____

d) D = {red but not jacks} = _____

   n(D) = _____

e) E = {face and black, but not queens}

   = _____

   n(E) = _____

f) F = {threes or spades but not hearts}

   = _____

   n(F) = _____

7.7) S = {those who like to play solitaire}, P = {those who like to play poker}, B = {those who like to play bridge}. Shade in the Venn diagram and describe the set using set notation.

a) those who like poker
   or solitaire

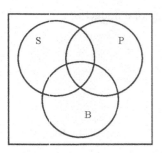

b) those who don't like poker

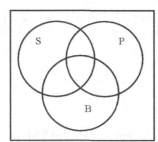

c) those who like bridge
   but not poker

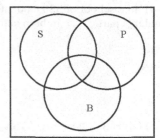

Set notation: _____   _____   _____

d) Using the same sets, S, P, and B, describe the shaded region and then put it in set notation (using unions, intersections, complements, etc).

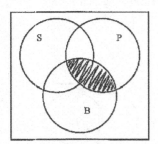

i) describe in words:

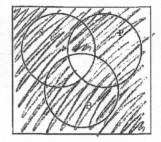

ii) describe in words:

iii) describe in words:

set notation _____   set notation _____   set notation _____

29

GROUP #8

Venn Diagrams

Draw Venn diagrams to answer the following:

8.1) Find $n(S \cap T)$, given that $n(S) = 4, n(T) = 12$, and $n(S \cup T) = 15$.

8.2) Find $n(T)$, given that $n(S) = 14, n(S \cap T) = 6$, and $n(S \cup T) = 17$.

8.3) In a class of 50 students, 18 play badminton, 26 play lawn bowling, and 2 play both badminton and lawn bowling. How many students in the class do not play either badminton or lawn bowling?

8.4) In a school of 320 students, 85 students are in the intramural kickball, 200 students are on intramural dodgeball, and 60 students participate in both activities. How many students are involved in kickball or dodgeball?

8.5) Given F = a set of 47 kids who like Freeze Tag and T = a set of 25 kids who like TV Tag, determine each of the following by drawing a Venn diagram for each of the situations:
   a) The maximum possible number of these kids who like Freeze Tag or TV Tag.
      [i.e. largest value for n(F ∪ T)]

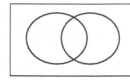

   b) The minimum possible number of these kids who like Freeze Tag or TV Tag.
      [i.e. smallest value for n(F ∪ T)]

   c) The maximum possible number of these kids who like both Freeze and TV Tag.
      [i.e. largest value for n(F ∩ T)]

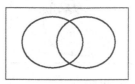

   d) The minimum possible number of these kids who like both Freeze and TV Tag.
      [i.e. smallest value for n(F ∩ T)]

8.6) You go to a barbeque with 26 guests and discover that 14 enjoy Frisbee, 10 enjoy Jumping Rope, and 5 enjoy Hopscotch. Four enjoy Frisbee and Jumping Rope, 3 enjoy Frisbee and Hopscotch, and one enjoys Jumping Rope and Hopscotch. If no one enjoys all three types of activities, how many guests do not enjoy any of these activities?

8.7) Twenty-five balls are in a bin in the backyard. Thirteen of the balls are black, six of the balls are flat, and fifteen of the balls have team logos on them. There is only one ball that is black and flat and has a logo. Two of the balls are black and flat and do not have logos. Two of the balls are flat and have logos but are not black. If all of the balls in the bin have at least one of the mentioned characteristics, how many balls are black and have logos but are not flat?

8.8) Illustrate the following on a Venn diagram:

$$n(A \cap B) = 6 \qquad n(A \cap B \cap C) = 4 \qquad n(A \cap C \cap B^c) = 3$$

$$n(B \cap C) = 4 \qquad n(A \cap C^c) = 11 \qquad n(C) = 15$$

$$n(A^c \cap B^c \cap C^c) = 5 \qquad n(B) = 12$$

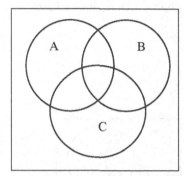

8.9) Fill in the Venn diagram with the following information and then answer the questions about children attending a HUGE birthday party:

    120 are girls
    150 like Pin the Tail on the Donkey
    170 like Musical Chairs
    100 of the boys don't like Musical Chairs
    108 of the boys like Pin the Tail on the Donkey
    18 of the girls who don't liked Pin the Tail on the Donkey, like Musical Chairs
    78 boys who don't like Pin the Tail on the Donkey don't like Musical Chairs either
    30 of the girls who liked Pin the Tail on the Donkey also like Musical Chairs

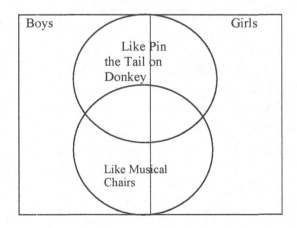

a) How many kids are at this birthday party?

b) How many attendees do not like Pin the Tail?

c) How many girls do not like Musical Chairs?

d) How many boys who like Musical Chairs like Pin the Tail on the Donkey?

31

8.10) Given that C = the set of kids who want to play Capture the Flag   n(C)=16
                        R = the set of kids who want to play Red Light Green Light   n(R) = 12
                        F = the set of kids who want to play Four Square   n(F) = 7,
   Draw a Venn diagram for each to determine the following:

a) The maximum number of kids who want to play Capture the Flag or Red Light
Green Light or Four Square. [i.e. largest value for n(C ∪ R ∪ F)]

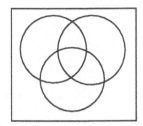

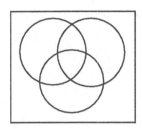

b) The minimum possible number of kids who want to play
Capture the Flag or Red Light Green Light or Four Square.
[i.e. smallest value for n(C ∪ R ∪ F)]

c) The maximum possible number of kids who want to play Capture the Flag and Red
Light Green Light and Four Square. [i.e. largest value for n(C ∩ R ∩ F)]

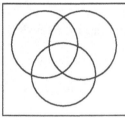

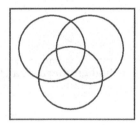

d) The minimum possible number of kids who want to
play Capture the Flag and Red Light Green Light and Four Square.
[i.e. smallest value for n(C ∩ R ∩ F)]

8.11) In a recent survey, consumers were asked where they shopped for sports equipment. The following results were
obtained: 213 shopped at Dick's Sporting Goods, 294 shopped at Play It Again Sports, and 337 shopped at Cabelas, 198
shopped at Play It Again and Cabelas, 382 shopped at Play It Again or Dick's, 61 shopped at Dick's and Cabelas but not at
Play It Again, 109 shopped at all three, and 64 shopped at neither Dick's nor Play It Again nor Cabelas. How many consumers

a) shopped at more than one of the stores?

b) shopped exclusively at Cabelas?

c) shopped at Dick's and Play It Again, but not Cabelas?

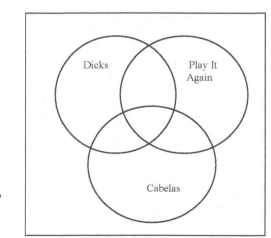

8.12) A survey of 136 arm chair athletes yielded the following information:

50 watched baseball   68 watched soccer
2 watch all 4   11 watch only football   14 watch only hockey
10 watch both football and hockey   21 watch both football and baseball
26 watch both hockey and soccer   27 watch both baseball and soccer
3 watch football, hockey, baseball, but not soccer   1 watches football, hockey, soccer, but not baseball
11 watch football, baseball, and soccer   12 watch hockey, baseball, and soccer

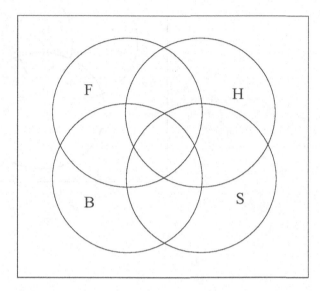

a) How many watch only soccer?

b) How many watch football or baseball?

c) How many watch none of these sports?

8.13) Given $n(A) = 98$ and $n(B) = 70$, determine each of the following by drawing a Venn diagram for each of the situations:

a) maximum of $n(A \cap B) = $ _____

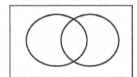

b) minimum of $n(A \cap B) = $ _____

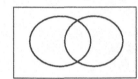

c) maximum of $n(A \cup B) = $ _____

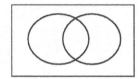

d) minimum of $n(A \cup B) = $ _____

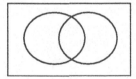

8.14) Given the Venn diagram and n(U) =19, determine the following:

a) $n(A \cup B)$ b) $n(A \cap B)$ c) $n(A)$ d) $n(B)$

e) $n(B \cap A^C)$ f) $n(B^C \cup A)$ g) $n(A \cup B)^C$ h) $n(A \cap B)^C$

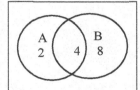

GROUP #9

More Venn Diagrams

A group of people are gathered where L is the set of all lacrosse players, S is the set of all soccer players, and B is the set of all baseball players.

9.1) State in words what each section of the Venn Diagram represents.

i)

ii)

iii)

iv)   viii)

v)   i + ii)

vi)   ii + v)

vii)   iii + v + vii)

9.2) Using set notation describe the sections:

i)   vii)

ii)   viii)

iii)   i + ii)

iv)   ii + v)

v)   iii + v + vii)

vi)

34

 **GROUP WORK** Your group will write 2 three circle Venn diagram problems. Be careful and make sure that you are giving enough information so your problem can be solved! (But don't make it too easy either.) You will trade with another group to see if your problems are solvable.

9.3) Create a three circle Venn diagram problem with a context (like problem 8.7) .

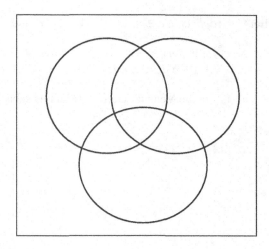

9.4) Create another three circle Venn diagram problem by just using numbers like n(A), etc (like problem 8.8).

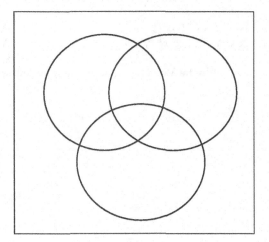

9.5) Let X and Y be subsets of U = {*a, b, c, d*, 1, 2, 3, 4}, X = {*a*, 2}, X ∩ Y = {2}, and X ∪ Y = {*a, b, d*, 2, 4}. Find Y.

9.6) Let U = {*a, b, c, d, e, f, g, h, i*} where X = {*a, c, f*}, X ∩ Y = {*f*}, and X ∪ Y = {*a, c, d, f, h*}. Find Y.

9.7) Let U = {*a, b, c, d, e, f, g, h, i, j*}. Let X, Y, and Z be subsets where:

X^C = {*b, d, f, h*}   Y ∪ Z = {*b, c, e, f, g, h, i*}   Y ∩ Z = {*g*}   X ∩ Y = {*c, e, g*}
X ∪ Y = {*a, b, c, e, g, i, j*} $Y^C ∩ Z^C$ = {*a, d, j*}   X ∩ Z = {*g, i*}.

a) Fill in the Venn diagram of U and its subsets.

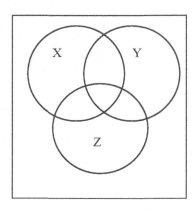

b) Find X.   c) Find Y.   d) Find Z.

9.8) Let U = {*a, b, c, d, e, f, g, h, i*}. Let X, Y, and Z be subsets where

X^C = {*a, b, f, g, i*}   Y ∪ Z = {*b, c, e, f, g, h*}   Y ∩ Z = {*f, h*}
X ∪ Y = {*b, c, d, e, f, h*} $Y^C ∩ Z^C$ = {*a, d, i*}   X ∩ Z = {*c, h*}.

a) Fill in the Venn diagram of U and its subsets.

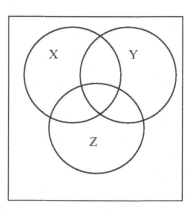

b) Find X.   c) Find Y.   d) Find Z.

Review problems:

9.9) In the game Bulls and Cows, a BULL = correct digit in the right position and a COW = correct digit in the wrong position. Determine the 3 digit code for each.

a)

Guess	# of Bulls	# of Cows
1 2 3	0	1
4 5 6	1	0
7 8 9	1	0
8 1 4	0	3

b)

Guess	# of Bulls	# of Cows
1 2 3	0	0
4 5 6	0	1
7 8 9	1	0
5 8 0	0	1
0 4 9	0	2

_____ _____ _____   _____ _____ _____

9.10) Let U = {a, b, c, d, e, f, g, h, i, j}. Given that A = {a, b, c, d, e}, B = {c, d, e, f, g, h}, and C = {a, f}, determine the following:

a) A^C = _____

b) $A \cap B$ = _____

c) $A \cup B$ = _____

d) $n(B)$ = _____

e) number of subsets of A = _____

f) $(B \cup C)^C$ = _____

g) list the subsets of C = _____

h) $(A \cup B)^C \cup C$ = _____

i) $\emptyset^C$ = _____

j) { } = $\emptyset$ True or false? _____

9.11) Determine how many cards are in the following sets:

a) H = {clubs or 6's}   b) K = {red and face}   c) V = {jacks or black, but not 8's}

$n(H)$ = _____ $n(K)$ = _____ $n(V)$ = _____

9.12) Let A represent those who like apples, B those who like bananas, and C those who like cantaloupe.

a) Describe the shaded area

i) using words.

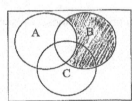

ii) using set notation.

b) Shade in the region in the Venn diagram and give the set notation:
   people who like apples or canteloupe but not bananas

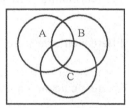

9.13) a) If you have 7 toppings, how many different pizzas can you make?

b) If you have a set with 10 elements, how many different subsets are possible?

GROUP #10

Is Order Important?

Discuss the following questions and decide if order makes a difference or not (just write YES if it does matter or NO). You don't have to figure out the actual answers (yet).

10.1) A university has three table tennis scholarships each worth $1000. How many ways are there to award these after they've narrowed the candidates to 6 ping pong players?

10.2) This same university has three badminton scholarships, one worth $3000, one worth $2000, and one worth $1000. If the field of qualified badminton candidates is also narrowed to 6, how many ways are there to give the scholarships?

10.3) How many ways are there for 8 teams in a soccer league to end the season in 1st, 2nd and 3rd place?

10.4) How many ways are there for 7 teams in a football league to end the season in the top three?

10.5) After being dealt five cards, how many different ways can a player arrange the cards in their hand?

10.6) How many different foursomes can be formed from among 6 golfers?

10.7) How many different finishes can occur in an 8-horse race (excluding the possibility of ties)?

10.8) How many different 9 player batting line ups are possible on a softball team with a 13-player roster?

10.9) How many different ways are there for a soccer team of 11 to choose 3 players to be team captains?

10.10) How many different 5 card poker hands are there?

10.11) How many different solutions are there for the game of Clue if the game has 9 rooms, 6 weapons, and 6 suspects?

10.12) How many different outcomes are there when you flip a penny three times in a row?

10.13) How many different outcomes are then when you flip three identical nickels at the same time?

10.14) How many different 2 card blackjack hands are there (first card dealt down, second dealt face up)?

10.15) In how many ways can 7 go-karts be situated on a circular track during a race, assuming that no two are exactly side by side?

10.16) How many ways are there to seat 4 people around a table to play Monopoly?

10.17) A 3 reel slot machine has 11 different symbols on each reel including one JACKPOT symbol. How many different ways could you get no JACKPOTs?

10.18) How many ways are there to grab 3 marbles at the same time out of a bag with 6 red marbles, 5 green marbles, and 2 blue marbles?

10.19) How many ways are there to grab 3 marbles one at a time out of that same bag so that the first is red, the second is green, and the third is blue?

10.20) How many different 3 piece ski outfits could you come up with if you have 2 jackets, 5 hats, and 4 pairs of gloves?

10.21) There are 100 squares on a Battleship game board. How many ways could you start off the game with your first, second, and third shot?

10.22) Uno is played with a deck of 108 Uno cards and everyone is dealt 7 cards. How many different Uno hands are there?

10.23) A family of 5 is playing on the game show Family Feud. How many different ways could they sit in a row to be asked questions?

10.24) Sixteen marching bands have volunteered to perform at the Lucas Oil Stadium during half time of a Colts game, but there in only enough for 10 of the bands to be on the field. How many ways are possible for the bands to be chosen?

10.25) A softball team consists of 7 adults and 6 teenagers. How many different ways can 2 captains be picked if there must be one adult and one teenager?

10.26) A hockey league has 15 teams. If every team must play every other team once in the first round of league play, how many games must be scheduled?

10.27) How many different "words" (can be nonsense words) can be formed using all of the letters in BIKE?

10.28) Given a group of 20 cheerleaders, 5 with megaphones and 15 without, how many ways can a group of 10 be picked to perform in a competition if there must be 7 without and 3 with megaphones?

10.29) You are playing Yahtzee and roll all 5 dice; how many different outcomes are possible?

10.30) There are 10 marbles in a bag, 5 green, 3 blue, and 2 red and you want to grab 3 of them, one at a time without replacement. How many ways are there to reach in and grab a green, and then a blue and then another green?

10.31) How many arrangements are there using all of the letters in INDIANA?

INTRO TO COMBINATORICS NOTES

COMBINATORICS is a branch of mathematics dealing with counting different outcomes of some task called an **experiment**.

A few definitions we will need in our study are as follows:

Experiment : an activity with an observable outcome   Ex1. roll a die

Sample Space S : the set of all of possible outcomes of an experiment Ex1. S =

Event E : subset of the sample space (some of the possible outcomes)

       Ex1. event : roll at least a 5   E =

n(A) = number of elements in the set A

       Ex1. n(S) =   n(E) =

Single-stage event: only one outcome (but may be several possible for this one outcome), for example Ex1.

Multi-stage event: experiments having two or more stages at which different outcomes occur, for example Ex2.

COUNTING ELEMENTS OF A SET

I. *Counting by Making a List*

One way to count outcomes is to **list** the elements (outcomes), but multi-stage events can be cumbersome to list all possible outcomes and know you have them all.

Ex2. Flip a coin three times in a row; event = tossing exactly two heads

       S =

       E =

II. *Counting with a Tree Diagram*

Yet another method to count outcomes that is a little more visual is to construct a **tree diagram** that can be especially useful for a multistage event such as Ex2. Make a tree diagram for flipping a coin three times in a row to find n(S).

Ex2.

III. *The Counting Principle*
If you were asked to make a tree diagram for flipping a coin 10 times, it would get a little out of hand. The **counting principle** would work much better. The counting principle states that in a multi-stage experiment, you can multiply the number of possible choices (or outcomes) at each stage together to get the total number of possible outcomes.

Ex2. Flip a coin 3 times in a row. Total number of possible outcomes =

Let's look at coin flipping more:

S = 4 flips of a coin   n(S) =

S = 5 flips of a coin   n(S) =

$\vdots$
$\vdots$

S = n flips of a coin   n(S) =

Ex3. You go out to dinner and have a choice of 6 appetizers, 10 main courses, and 5 desserts. How many different three course meals are possible?

Ex4. A disc golf team is going cheap to number their jerseys- they found a bunch of iron-on 1's, 2's, 6's, 7's, and 8's. How many two-digit numbers can be made if
    a) repetition is allowed?   b) repetition is not allowed?

    c) only odd two-digit numbers can be used (repetition not allowed)?

HOMEWORK PROBLEMS:

1) How many three-digit numbers can be made from the digits 1, 2, 3, 4, 5, 9 if
    a) repetition is allowed?   b) repetition is not allowed?

    c) number must be even and repetition is not allowed?   d) number must be odd and repetition is allowed?

2) A soccer store offers 4 choices of shin-guards, 8 different soccer shoes, and 5 different soccer balls for kids. How many different ways are there to outfit a child at this store?

3) A college is looking for a new football coach and a new swimming coach. In how many ways can the positions be filled if there are three applicants for the football position and four for the swimming position?

4) Your team decides to buy your dodge ball coach a gift at the end of the season. Your coach likes word games (Scrabble, Boggle, or Wheel of Fortune), old video games (PacMan or Ms. PacMan), and candy (M&M's or Snickers), so you decide to all chip in and buy one of each. Draw a tree to determine how many different gifts your team could give your coach and then use the Fundamental Principle of Counting to verify.

5) How many different sequences of heads and tails are possible if a coin is flipped 8 times?

6) How many 3 digit numbers (not starting with 0) are there which are not divisible by 5?

7) In the locker room after practice, you can't remember your combination. If it consists of 5 single digit numbers (0-9), how many different combinations are possible for you to try?

8) A sporting goods store has fourteen lines of snow skis, seven types of bindings, nine types of boots, and three types of poles. Assuming that all items are compatible with each other, how many different complete ski equipment packages are available?

9) You have 9 different skateboard stickers all of which would fit on your skateboard at once. How many different ways could you decorate your skateboard- using all of the stickers, some of the stickers, or none?

10) On their way to a Pacers game, how many ways can a family of five be seated in a car if either two or three people sit in the front seat and only two members of the family can drive?

11) A high school offers 6 varsity sports in the fall, 3 in the winter, and 5 in the spring. How many different 3 sport athletes could there be at this high school?

12) How many four-digit numbers (meaning they don't start with a 0) are there that do not contain a 5?

13) A *trifecta* in horse racing consists of choosing the exact order of the first three horses across the finish line. If there are 6 horses in the race, how many different trifectas are possible, assuming there are no ties?

14) How many ways can a child get in and then out of a 4 door car if they need to enter and exit through different doors?

15) There are four polo teams in a league. How many different orders are there for them to end the season?

16) A pizza store offers 20 toppings. How many different pizzas can you order?

17) How many 3 digit numbers less than 500 can be formed from 2, 4, 6, and 8 if repetition of digits is allowed?

18) How many numbers (any length) less than 500 can be formed from 2, 4, 6, and 8 if repetition of digits is allowed?

19) How many different license plates can a state issue with 3 letters followed by 3 digits if repetition is not allowed?

20) How many different outcomes are there when you roll a pair of dice?

21) If you flip a coin 4 times in a row, how many different ways can you get
    a) no tails?   b) 1 tail?   c) 2 tails?

    d) 3 tails?   e) 4 tails?

22) How many different outcomes are there when you flip a coin 4 times in a row?

23) General postal zip codes are 5 digits long.
    a) How many different zip codes are there is repetition is allowed?

    b) If letters are used instead of digits in a new zip code, how long would this new code need to be to make as many zip codes as five digits?

GROUP #11

 **Poker Chips**

Each group has a bag of different colored poker chips. For each question below rearrange the chips to determine the answers. Use **B** for blue, **R** for red, **W** for white, and **M** for maroon.

11.1) Use three different colored chips from the bag. **LIST THE OUTCOMES** and the total number of ways for each.

a) How many ways are there to grab one chip?

Total number: _____

b) How many ways are there to grab a 1st chip and then a 2nd chip without replacement?

Total number: _____

c) How many ways are there to grab a 1st chip, then a 2nd, and then a 3rd without replacement?

Total number: _____

d) How many ways are there to grab 2 of the 3 chips at once?

Total number: _____

e) How many ways are there to grab all 3 chips at once?

Total number: _____

f) How many ways are there to put the chips in a circle?

Total number: _____

11.2) Now use four different colored chips. **LIST THE OUTCOMES** and the total number of ways for each.

a) How many ways are there to grab one chip?

Total number: _____

b) How many ways are there to grab a 1st chip and then a 2nd chip without replacement?

Total number: _____

c) How many ways are there to grab a 1st chip, then a 2nd chip, and then a 3rd chip without replacement? Just list the outcomes with the red chip R being the 1st chip grabbed and extrapolate the total.

Total number: _____

d) How many ways are there to order the four chips in a row? You don't have to list them all, but using c) tell how you could easily get all of the ways.

Total number: _____

e) How many ways are there to choose 2 of the 4 chips at once?

Total number: _____

f) How many ways are there to choose 3 of the 4 chips at once?

Total number: _____

g) How many ways are there to choose all 4 chips at once?

Total number: _____

h) How many ways are there to put the chips in a circle?

Total number: _____

11.3) For these problems, take both blue chips (B1 and B2) and all three white chips (W1, W2, and W3) out, so you'll have 5 chips total. **LIST THE OUTCOMES** and the total number for each. For all of these order doesn't matter; you grab the chips at the same time.

a) How many ways are there to grab one chip?

Total number: _____

b) How many ways are there to choose 2 blue chips?

Total number: _____

c) How many ways are there to choose 2 white chips?

Total number: _____

d) How many ways are there to choose 1 blue and 1 white?

Total number: _____

45

e) How many ways are there to choose 2 chips?

Total number: _____

f) How many ways are there to choose 2 blue and 1 white?

Total number: _____

g) How many ways are there to choose 1 blue and 2 white?

Total number: _____

h) How many ways are there to choose 3 chips?

Total number: _____

i) How many ways are there to choose 4 chips?

Total number: _____

j) How many ways are there to choose 5 chips?

Total number: _____

11.4) For these last problems, take out the 2 blue chips, 2 white chips, and 1 red chip. We will NOT be distinguishing the numbers on the blue and white chips. For each of the following problems, order does matter and you grab the chips one at a time without replacement. Again, **LIST THE OUTCOMES**.

a) Using 2 blue and 1 white, how many ways are there to grab a 1st, 2nd, and 3rd chip?

Total number: _____

b) Using 2 blue and 2 white, how many ways are there to grab a 1st, 2nd, 3rd, and 4th chip?

Total number: _____

c) Using 2 blue, 1 white, and 1 red, how many ways are there to grab the chips in a row?

Total number: _____

Counting Principle Review: Here are a few problems referring back to the game Bulls and Cows (remember, n-digit codes that you had to guess).

11.5) How many different 3 digit codes are there if
      a) repetition is not allowed?   b) repetition is allowed?

      c) the code number must be even and repetition is not allowed?

      d) the code number must be odd and repetition is allowed?

11.6) How many different 4 digit codes are there if
      a) repetition is not allowed?   b) repetition is allowed?

      c) the code number must be even and repetition is allowed?

      d) the code number cannot have any 0s or 1s and repetition is not allowed?

11.7) How about 5 digit codes if
      a) repetition is not allowed?   b) repetition is allowed?

      c) the code number must start with an 8, end with a 4, and repetition is not allowed?

      d) the code number must be odd but cannot have any 5s in it and repetition is not allowed?

11.8) How many 6 digit codes are there if 0 must be in the code and repetition is not allowed?

PERMUTATIONS AND COMBINATIONS NOTES

FACTORIALS $n! = n\,(n-1)\,(n-2)\ldots(3)\,(2)\,(1)$

$0! =$ $1! =$ $2! =$ $3! =$ $4! =$ $5! =$ $\ldots 10! =$

PERMUTATIONS: ordered arrangements of objects (**distinguishable**) ORDER MATTERS!!!

$nPr = P(n, r) =$

Ex1. If a family of six decides to bowl on their Wii but only have four Wii remotes, how many orders are there for four members of the family to bowl?

Ex2. a) If there are 10 women in a tennis tournament, how many ways are there for them to finish the tournament in 1st, 2nd, and 3rd?

   b) What if there were 100 women in the tournament and we wanted to know how many ways for them to finish in $1^{st} - 10^{th}$ place?

Ex3. Eleven people, consisting of 5 men, 2 women, and 4 kids, are going to a Butler basketball game and have 11 seats in a row. How many ways are there to seat them if:
   a) no restrictions?

   b) the grown-ups sit together and the kids sit together?

   c) the women sit together, the men sit together, and the kids sit together?

PERMUTATIONS of Objects with some being Identical: If there are n objects of r different types of objects, where k_1 identical objects of one type, k_2 of another type, etc, then the number of different permutations is:

$$\frac{n!}{k_1!\cdot k_2!\cdots k_r!} \quad \text{where } k_1 + k_2 + \cdots + k_r = n$$

Ex4. How many different arrangements of all of the letters in the word AARDVARK are there?

CIRCULAR PERMUTATIONS: to seat n people in a circle, there are **(n-1)!** ways

 Ex5. If Brad invites 4 of his friends over to play poker one Friday night, how many ways are for the 5 to sit at Brad's round poker table?

COMBINATIONS: Order does NOT matter   nCr = C(n, r) =   use nCr key on calculator

 Ex6. Of the 10 women in a tennis tournament, how many ways are there for the players to finish in the top three?

 Ex7. Let's say a group of 11 people (consisting of 5 men, 2 women, and 4 kids) only have 6 tickets for an Indiana Fuel hockey game. How many ways are there for them to choose who gets to go to the game if:
  a) no restrictions?   b) 2 men, 1 woman, and 3 kids get to go?

  c) exactly 3 men get to go?

  d) at least 2 kids get to go?

HOMEWORK PROBLEMS

1) Using a standard deck of 52 cards, how many different ten card hands are possible?

2) There are 10 different representatives.
  a) How many ways can they be introduced at a meeting?

  b) How many ways can they sit around a table?

3) How many ways can twelve people be divided into hockey teams of six players each?

4) From 5 Sorry players, 4 Chutes and Ladders players, and 3 Uno players (12 players total), a committee of 6 is to be chosen. In how many ways can this be done with:

a) no restrictions?

b) 3 Sorry, 2 Chutes and Ladders, and 1 Uno player?

c) exactly 2 are Uno players?

d) at least four are Sorry players?

5) In a chess club consisting of sixteen members, how many ways are there of choosing a committee of seven if

a) no restrictions?

b) the president must be on the committee and another member is not able to serve?

6) In how many ways can three bowlers be selected out of fifteen if:

a) there are no restictions?

b) one of the bowlers is included in every selection?

c) two of the bowlers are to be excluded from every selection?

d) one is always included and two are always excluded?

7) How many 10-card hands can be dealt containing exactly 8 red cards?

8) How many distinguishable arrangements are there of the letters in each of the following words?

a) PUPPY

b) BUTLER

c) GIGGLING

d) MISSISSIPPI

9) From a standard deck, how many five-card hands containing only face cards can be dealt?

10) How many 5-card hands dealt from a standard deck of cards will have no clubs?

11) From a league of 7 track and field teams, how many ways can they end the season:
      a) in 1st, 2nd, and 3rd place?   b) in the top three?

12) How many ways 4 digit numbers can be constructed from the digits {1, 2, 3, 4, 5, 6, 7} if repetition is allowed?

13) In how many ways can three girls and two boys on a co-ed volleyball team be introduced before a game, given the following conditions?
      a) there are no restrictions   b) the boys go before the girls

      c) girls together and boys together   d) the boys and girls alternate

14) How many different lottery tickets can you choose of the following? (Order is not important and numbers don't repeat)
      a) Choosing five of the numbers 1 through 36.   b) Choosing six numbers from 1 to 53.

      c) Which lottery would be easier to win? Why?

15) If there are 4 blue pens and 5 red pens in a cup, how many ways can you grab 3 of them and get at most 1 red?

16) How many ways can a group of 15 people get a
      a) committee of 4?   b) a president, vp, secretary, and treasurer?

17) A softball league has 14 teams. If every team must play every other team once in the first round of league play, how many games must be scheduled?

18) If you have 4 identical quarters, 5 identical dimes, 2 identical nickels, and 3 identical pennies, how many different ways could you stack your coins?

19) Two hundred people buy raffle tickets. Three winning tickets will be drawn at random.
    a) If first prize is $100, second is $50, and third is $20, in how many different ways can the prizes be awarded?

    b) If each prize is $50, in how many ways can the prizes be awarded?

20) There are 4 fans who will sit in 6 seats in a row at a Colts game. In how many ways can the fans be seated?

21) You have 4 dogs, 2 cats, and 3 guinea pigs and they all need to go to the vet. How many ways are there to make appointments for them with
    a) no restrictions?   b) the dogs go first, the cats go next, and the guinea pigs go last?

    c) the dogs have consecutive appointments, the cats have consecutive appointments and the guinea pigs have consecutive appointments but in any order?

    d) Now there are only 5 time slots at the vet. How many ways can some of the animals make appointments if
        i) no restrictions?

        ii) the appointments are specifinally ordered 2 dogs, then 1 cat, and then 2 guinea pigs?

22) How many different 9 digit social security numbers are there with
    a) no restrictions?   b) exactly eight 0s?

    c) exactly six 0's and no 7s?

23) How many ways can 2 cans of Coke, 3 cans of Sprite, and 3 cans of Crush be distributed among 8 students?

Is Order Important? II
Crunching the Numbers

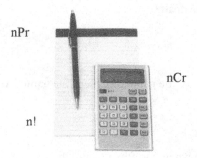

nPr

nCr

n!

We already discussed in groups if order was important, so use this knowledge and what we know about combinatorics, permutations and combinations to determine the answers to the following questions. MAKE SURE TO SHOW YOUR WORK, NOT JUST GIVE AN ANSWER (use factorials and nCr, etc).

12.1) A university has three table tennis scholarships each worth $1000. How many ways are there to award these after they've narrowed the candidates to 6 ping pong players?

12.2) This same university has three badminton scholarships, one worth $3000, one worth $2000, and one worth $1000. If the field of qualified badminton candidates is also narrowed to 6, how many ways are there to give the scholarships?

12.3) How many ways are there for 8 teams in a soccer league to end the season in 1st, 2nd and 3rd place?

12.4) How many ways are there for 7 teams in a football league to end the season in the top three?

12.5) After being dealt five cards, how many different ways can a player arrange the cards in their hand?

12.6) How many different foursomes can be formed from among 6 golfers?

12.7) How many different finishes can occur in an 8-horse race (excluding the possibility of ties)?

12.8) How many different 9 player batting line ups are possible on a softball team with a 13-player roster?

12.9) How many different ways are there for a soccer team of 11 to choose 3 players to be team captains?

12.10) How many different 5 card hands can be dealt?

12.11) How many different solutions are there for the game of Clue if the game has 9 rooms, 6 weapons, and 6 suspects?

12.12) How many different outcomes are there when you flip a penny three times in a row?

12.13) How many different outcomes are then when you flip three identical nickels at the same time?

12.14) How many different 2-card blackjack hands can be dealt with first card dealt down, second dealt face up?

12.15) In how many ways can 7 go-karts be situated on a circular track during a race, assuming that no two are exactly side by side?

12.16) How many ways are there to seat 4 people around a table to play bridge?

12.17) A 3 reel slot machine has 10 different symbols on each reel (including one JACKPOT symbol). How many different outcomes are there for this slot machine?

12.18) How many ways are there to grab 3 marbles out of a bag with 6 red marbles, 5 green marbles, and 2 blue marbles?

12.19) How many ways are there to grab 3 marbles out of that same bag so that the first is red, the second is green, and the third is blue?

12.20) How many different 3 piece ski outfits could you come up with if you have 2 jackets, 5 hats, and 4 pairs of gloves?

12.21) There are 100 squares on a Battleship game board. How many ways could you start off the game with your first, second, and third shot?

12.22) Uno is played with a deck of 108 Uno cards and everyone is dealt 7 cards. How many different Uno hands are there?

12.23) A family of 5 is playing on the game show Family Feud. How many different ways could they sit in a row to be asked questions?

12.24) Sixteen marching bands have volunteered to perform at the Lucas Oil Stadium during half time of a Colts game, but there in only enough space for 10 of the bands to be on the field. How many ways are possible for the bands to be chosen?

12.25) A coed softball team consists of 7 women and 6 men. How many different ways can 2 captains be picked if there must be one man and one woman?

12.26) A hockey league has 15 teams. If every team must play every other team once in the first round of league play, how many games must be scheduled?

12.27) How many different "words" (can be nonsense words) can be formed using all of the letters in BIKE?

12.28) Given a group of 20 cheerleaders, 15 females and 5 males, how many ways can a group of 10 be picked to perform in a competition if there must be 7 females and 3 males?

12.29) You are playing Yahtzee and roll all 5 dice; how many different outcomes are possible?

12.30) There are 10 marbles in a bag, 5 green, 3 blue, and 2 red and you want to grab 3 of them, one at a time without replacement. How many ways are there to reach in and grab a green, and then a blue and then another green?

12.31) How many arrangements are there using all of the letters in INDIANA?

For the next two problems, you are the coach of a baseball team called the Strikers which has 12 kids (7 boys and 5 girls) on it. Make sure you show work on these problems to show how you're getting your answer.

12.32) Positions

a) How many different ways are there to rest three of the players when your team is out in the field?

b) After you've chosen your three who will rest, how many ways are there to assign your remaining nine players to either the outfield (3) or the infield (6) where their actual positions are not important, only infield or outfield?

c) How many ways can you assign the three selected for outfield to right/left/ or center?

d) And the six in the infield (1st, 2nd, 3rd, shortstop, catcher, and pitcher)?

e) The league has a rule that at least 4 girls must be playing in the field. How many ways can you assign nine of the players from the 12 to play the field (no positions)?

f) Let's say you've chosen your nine to play on the field consisting of all 5 girls. How many ways can you assign the nine players to the outfield or infield if exactly 3 of the boys must be in the infield?

12.33) Batting Order

a) How many different nine person line ups are there?

b) How many different nine person line ups are there if it must alternate 1st a girl, boy, girl, boy, etc.?

c) You want your fastest base runner to lead off and your star hitter to be in the clean-up position (4th), how many line ups are there?

d) What if you have in mind the top 4 batters whom you would like to be at the top of the batting order (but not their order) and then fill in the remaining 5 spots?

GROUP #13

Poker Hands
and Combinations

When most people think of poker, they think of straight poker which is played with each player dealt 5 cards. In this group project we will be using combinatorics to count the number of different types of 5 card poker hands. Note that order doesn't matter; a poker hand is the same no matter how you were dealt your cards.

13.1) How many different 5 card poker hands are there?

How many 5 card poker hands are there with the following properties:

13.2) all red?

13.3) no red?

13.4) all hearts?

13.5) exactly 3 black?

13.6) no clubs?

13.7) 3 black and 2 diamonds?

13.8) 2 spades and 3 hearts?

13.9) 1 club and 4 spades?

13.10) exactly 2 hearts?

13.11) exactly 4 spades?

13.12) at least 4 black?

13.13) at most 1 heart?

13.14) at least 4 clubs?

13.15) 3 jacks and 2 eights?

13.16) 4 tens and 1 ace?

13.17) 4 aces?

13.18) at most 1 six?

13.19) exactly 3 fives?

13.20) all face cards?

13.21) no aces?

13.22) at least one ace?

13.23) exactly 2 face cards?

13.24) contains ace of ♠?

13.25) does not contain ace of ♠?

13.26) contains ace of ♠ but no hearts?

13.27) contains two aces and no queens?

13.28) contains no jacks, no queens, but all of the kings?

13.29) four of a kind (4 of a rank and one singleton)?

13.30) all of the same suit (i.e. a flush)?   13.31) an ace, 2, 3, 4, and 5?

More Combinatorics problems

13.32) You have 4 toppings (pepperoni, mushroom, onion, and green pepper) in your refrigerator and want to make pizza. How many different pizzas can you make with:

      a) only 1 topping?   b) 2 toppings?

      c) 3 toppings?   d) 4 toppings?

      e) So how many total different pizzas can you make with 4 toppings in your fridge? (Remember there's always a plain cheese pizza as well.)

      f) What's another way to get the total number of pizzas?

13.33) You have a test that has 5 true false questions on it.
      a) How many different ways are there to answer all 5 questions?

      b) How many ways are there to get
          i) 5 correct?   ii) 4 correct?

          iii) 3 correct?   iv) no questions correct?

13.34) Think about dealing with **n** experiments that each have two outcomes. Coin flipping with heads/tails, pizza toppings that are either off/on, questions that are either true/false, and elements are either in/out of subsets are some examples.
      a) How many different total outcomes are there for these types of problems where there are **n** things each with two outcomes?

      b) If you only want **r** of the **n** things to be one of the two outcomes (say heads for coin flipping), how many different ways are there for this?

GROUP #14

Volleyball Tournaments

You are on a volleyball team called the Spikers and your team plays in many tournaments, including single elimination, double elimination, best of three, and best of five. In this group, you will determine how many games will be played in each type of tournament with a given number of teams.

14.1) Your team is entered in a single elimination tournament (meaning one loss and your team is out). State how many total games will be played during the tournament. Think of how many losses have to take place.
    a) 4 teams total   b) 8 teams total   c) 12 teams total

    d) 100 teams total   e) If there are N teams, how many games would need to be played?

14.2) You've entered your team in a double elimination tournament which means you get 2 losses before your team is out. State how many total games will be played during the tournament. Again, think of how many losses must take place. Note that there will be two answers for each scenario.
    a) 2 teams total   b) 3 teams total   c) 11 teams total

    d) 91 teams total   e) If there are N teams, how many games would need to be played?

    f) Why are there two answers for each scenario?

14.3) Now your team is in a triple elimination tournament which means you get 3 losses before your team is out. Think about losses again and how many different outcomes you will have for each scenario
    a) 2 teams total   b) 6 teams total   c) 11 teams total

    d) 91 teams total   e) If there are N teams, how many games would need to be played?

14.4) Let's say the Spikers make it to the league championship which is a Best of Three series (first team to win 2 games, wins). They will be playing the Diggers. Note that there will either be 2 or 3 games played.

a) Draw a tree diagram to show how the series could end. Each branch will represent the team who wins each game. Start with game 1 either the Spikers (S) will win or the Diggers (D), then the next game, etc. Stop once a team has won 2 games.

b) List the possible outcomes for this best of three series by following each branch to the end, noting who won each of the games.

14.5) Now let's say the Spikers and Diggers are playing a Best of Five series (first team to win 3 games wins the series, so there could be 3, 4, or 5 games played).

a) Draw a tree diagram to represent the possibilities. Hint: This tree will be much bigger with 20 possible outcomes, so you only have to draw half of the tree.

b) List the possible outcomes for this Best of Five series. (Again you only need to do half of them.)

14.6) The Spikers have entered a round robin tournament which is one where every team plays every other team once.

    a) How many games would be played with 2 other teams (3 total)?

    b) How many games with 3 other teams (4 total)?

    c) How about 4 others teams (5 total)?

    d) Can you come up with a formula to determine the number of games for N teams in a round robin tournament?

14.7) Then look on the internet and find an example of leagues that use the formats and how they use them (for example Major League Baseball uses a best of seven series for the World Series- you can't use that example now!).

    a) **Best of three series**: Two teams play 2 or 3 games; whoever wins 2 games first wins the series.

        example:

    b) **Best of five series**: Two teams play 3, 4, or 5 games; whoever wins 3 games first wins the series.

        example:

    c) **Best of seven series:** Two teams play (A and B) 4, 5, 6, or 7 games; first to win four games wins the series. There are 70 possible outcomes for a Best of Seven series, so you only need to list 2 possible outcomes of each where 4, 5, 6, and 7 games had to be played to determine the winner (example: for 6 games you could use AABABA, but you can't use that now I've used it!).

4 games: 6 games:

5 games: 7 games:

        example:

14.8) The NCAA basketball tournament is a single elimination tournament at the end of the season and allows 68 teams in; how many games are played?

14.9) How many games would there be if the NCAA basketball tourney were a double elimination tournament with 68 teams?

14.10) If you are entered in a quadruple elimination tournament (lose 4 games and your team is out), how many different games would be played with:

    a) 5 teams?   b) 11 teams?   c) N teams?

REVIEW PROBLEMS FOR TEST 1

1) Determine the surnames of four people, their position in a cake-bake competition and what cake they baked.

   The first names are: *James, Ben, Vicky* and *Nigel*
   The surnames are: *Jones, Stevens, Andrews* and *Best*
   Positions are: *1st, 2nd, 3rd* and *4th*
   Cakes baked are: *chocolate cake, cheese cake, fruit cake* and *sponge cake*.

   1. James Best beat Vicky by two places.
   2. Ben's fruit cake beat Mrs. Stevens' son, who came in 3rd.
   3. The sponge cake, despite being a bit bland, got in the top three.
   4. The judges obviously had a sweet tooth, as the chocolate cake came in 2nd place.
   5. Jones's mother cried as she watched her son take 1st prize.

   What are the full names of the top four, what position did they come and what cake did they bake?

position	1st	2nd	3rd	4th
first name				
surname				
cake				

2) Use set notation to describe the shaded region.

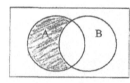

3) Given the sets: $U = \{1,2,3,4,5,6,7\}$, $A = \{3,4,5,6\}$, $B = \{1,2\}$, $C = \{1,3,5,7\}$, and $D = \{7\}$, determine the following:

a) TRUE or FALSE $A^C = B \cup D$

h) TRUE or FALSE $A = \{4,6,3,5\}$

b) list the subsets of $D =$ _____

i) $\{2\}$____B fill in with $\in$ or $\subseteq$

c) TRUE or FALSE $\emptyset \subseteq D$

j) TRUE or FALSE $\emptyset \not\subseteq U$

d) $(B \cup C) \cap A =$ _____

k) TRUE or FALSE $\emptyset = \{\emptyset\}$

e) the number of subsets of $C =$ _____

l) TRUE or FALSE $B \subseteq C$

f) $U^c =$ _____

m) $(B \cup D)^c \cap C =$ _____

g) $A \cup C =$ _____

n) $n(A \cup C) =$ _____

4) Given $n(L) = 570$, $n(L \cup M) = 700$, $n(L \cap M) = 60$, find $n(M)$.

5) The management of a hotel conducted a survey and found that of the 2560 guests who were surveyed,

1780 tip the wait staff   700 tip the wait staff and the maids
1200 tip the luggage handlers   750 tip the wait staff and the luggage handlers
830 tip the maids   200 tip all three services
80 tip the maids and the luggage handlers but not the wait staff

Fill in the VENN DIAGRAM completely and answer the following: How many of the guests tip:

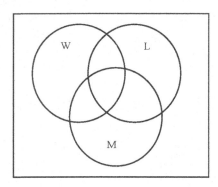

a) exactly two of the services?   b) the wait staff or the maids?

c) maids or luggage handlers but not wait staff?   d) do not tip any?

6) Shade the region on the Venn diagram that represents $A \cup B^C$.

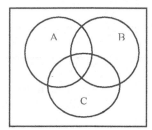

7) Fill in the sudoku.

2					1
	5	1		3	
			4		5
	6				
3			6	2	
	4				

8) Nine individuals - Z, Y, X, W, V, U, T, S and R - are the only candidates, who can serve on three committees-- A, B and C, and each candidate should serve on exactly one of the committees.

Committee A should consist of exactly one member more than committee B.
It is possible that there are no members of committee C, but A and B must have at least one member each.
Z, Y and X can NOT serve on committee A.
W, V and U can NOT serve on committee B.
T, S and R can NOT serve on committee C.

a) If T and Z are the only ones serving on committee B, how many of the 9 individuals should serve on committee C?

b) Of the nine individuals, the largest number that can serve together on committee C is

c) If T, S and X are the only individuals serving on committee B, who should be on committee C?

9) There are 11 people on a committee. How many ways are there for them to:
   a) elect a president, vice president, and secretary?   b) choose a subcommittee of 3?

10) How many five card hands dealt from standard deck of cards will have:
   a) all spades?   b) 3 tens and 2 face cards?

   c) 2 queens but no hearts?   d) at least 4 of the cards are black?

11) From 5 physicists, 4 chemists, and 3 mathematicians a committee of 6 is to be chosen. How many ways can this be done if:
   a) there are no restrictions?   b) 3 physicists, 2 chemists, and 1 mathematician?

   c) exactly 2 mathematicians?   d) at most one are physicists?

12) A cafeteria offers 2 choices of meat, 4 choices of veggies, 3 choices of drink, and 6 choices of fruit. How many 4-item lunches are available?

13) How many *three* digit numbers are possible from the digits 1, 2, 4, 6, 7, 8 if repetition:
   a) is allowed?   b) is not allowed?

   c) is not allowed and the number must be even?   d) is allowed and the number must be odd?

14) In the game Bulls and Cows, a BULL = correct digit in the right position and a COW = correct digit in the wrong position. Determine the code for the example.

Guess 1: 123	→	1 bull and 0 cows
Guess 2: 456	→	0 bulls and 1 cow
Guess 3: 789	→	0 bulls and 0 cow
Guess 4: 140	→	0 bulls and 1 cow
Guess 5: 025	→	0 bulls and 2 cows

Code: ____ ____ ____

15) How many games would be played in a tournament with 14 teams which is:
    a) single elimination?   b) double elimination?

16) Given a standard deck of cards, find n(A) for each set:
    a) A={clubs and red}   b) A={nines or spades}   c) A={twos or hearts, but not fours}

17) You have 12 books, consisting of 4 historical fictions, 5 mysteries, and 3 nonfictions. How many ways are there to put them on one shelf with:
    a) no restrictions?   b) the mysteries are all on the left?

    c) similar types are shelved together?

18) You flip a penny 7 times in a row.
    a) How many different outcomes are possible?

    b) How many different outcomes consist of exactly 3 tails?

19) How many different games must be played if a field hockey league with 6 teams if every team must play every other team?

20) Let A be the people who like apples, B those who like bananas, and C those who like cantaloupe. Given the Venn, describe the shaded region:

a) in words

b) using set notation

66

TEST 2

Probability

INTRO TO PROBABILITY NOTES

PROBABILITY is a branch of mathematics that studies the likelihood that a certain event will occur. Probability is a continuation of combinatorics, so we will use the same terminology.

PROBABILITY OF EVENT E:
$$P(E) = \frac{n(E)}{n(S)} = \frac{\#\ of\ elements\ in\ E}{total\ \#\ of\ possible\ outcomes}$$

PROPERTIES OF PROBABILITIES:

    1) $0 \leq P(E) \leq 1$ all probabilities must be between 0.0 and 1.0 (0% and 100%)

    2) if $P(E) = 1$ then E always happens (100% of the time)

    3) if $P(E) = 0$ then E never happens (0% of the time)

Ex1. Draw one card from a deck

    P(♦) =   P(3♠) =   P(face card) =

Ex2. Flip a coin three times

    P(2 heads) =   P(1 tail) =   P(at least 2 H) =

Ex3. Flip a coin ten times.

    P(6 heads) =   P(at most 1 tail) =

ODDS in favor of event E are **a to b** (or **a:b**) means every **a** times event E occurs, **b** times event E does not occur.
Odds **against** event E are then just **b to a**.

Think in terms of event E occurring as a WIN and event E not occurring as a LOSS; then odds in favor are in terms of WINS to LOSSES (a to b). Then odds against E occurring are LOSSES TO WINS (b to a).

Ex1. There are 2 pink, 4 green, and 5 blue marbles in a bag and you reach in and grab one.

    Odds in favor of getting a green marble _____ to _____

    P(grabbing a green) =

Odds in favor of E are **a:b**, then $P(E) = \frac{a}{a+b}$

Ex2

Probability of E occurring	Odds in favor of E occurring	Odds against E occurring
$P(E) = \frac{a}{a+b}$	a to b	b to a
$\frac{5}{17}$		
	8 to 3	

Ex3. A fair die is rolled, what are the odds in favor of rolling an even #?

Ex4. In a contest, the odds against winning 1st prize are 100 to 1, what is the probability of winning?

MUTUALLY EXCLUSIVE: events that can't occur at the same time $A \cap B = \emptyset$ which means that:

$$P(A \ or \ B) = P(A \cup B) = P(A) + P(B)$$

Ex1. P(rolling a 3 or a 4)   Ex2. P(draw a ♠ or red card)

ADDITION RULE FOR PROBABILITIES for any event A and B, $P(A \cup B) = P(A) + P(B) - P(A \cap B)$

Ex1. Given $P(A) = 0.6, P(B) = 0.5$, and $P(A \cap B) = 0.2$; then find $P(A \cup B)$.

Ex2. P(drawing a 3 or ♥) =

Ex3. Two cards are drawn from a deck.

   a) P(both are black or both are hearts)   b) P(both are hearts or both are face)

Ex4. A bag contains 2 blue, 3 red, and 4 white poker chips and three are chosen at random at the same time.

   a) P(2 are white)   b) P(no white)

   c) P(at least one white)

COMPLEMENT E^c for event E, $$P(E^C) = 1 - P(E)$$

The idea is that the probability of an event happening plus the probability of the event not happening equals one.

NOTE: P(at least one _____) = 1 – P(no _____)

Ex. You flip a coin 4 times.

    a) P(at least 1 tail)   b) P(at least 3 tails)

HOMEWORK PROBLEMS:

1) A gym lock has a disk with 36 numbers written around its edge. The combination to the lock is made up of three numbers (such as 12-33-07) with repetition allowed.
    a) How many different possible combinations are there for this lock?

    b) What is the probability of randomly guessing the correct one?

2) What is the probability of seeing exactly 3 heads when a coin is tossed five times?

3) You flip a nickel 13 times in a row.
    a) P(4 tails)   b) P(at most 3 tails)

4) A letter is chosen randomly from the alphabet. What's the probability that letter is in the word CRIBBAGE or YAHTZEE?

5) A bookmaker has placed 8 to 3 odds against a particular football team winning its next game. What is the probability, in the bookmaker's view, of the team winning?

6) In March 2004, vegas.com gave odds on who would win the 2004 World Series. They gave the New York Yankees 2:1 odds and the Boston Red Sox 5:2 odds.
    a) Find the probabilities that each of the teams will win according to these odds.

    b) Who did they think was more likely to win the World Series?

7) One card is drawn from a deck.
    a) What are the odds of getting a 7?

    b) What are the odds against getting a face card?

    c) What are the odds in favor of getting a jack or red card?

    d) What are the odds against getting a club and face but not a queen?

8) The game board for the television show Jeopardy is divided into six categories with each category containing 5 answers. In the Double Jeopardy round, there are two hidden Daily Double squares.
    a) What is the probability that a contestant chooses a Daily Double square on the first turn?

    b) What are the odds in favor of choosing a Daily Double square on the first turn?

9) From a deck of cards, you turn over a 5 and then a 6. What is the probability the next card you turn over will be a:
    a) face card?   b) another 5?

10) The lottery in an extremely small state consists of picking two different numbers from 1 to 10. Ten numbered ping pong balls are dropped in a fish bowl and two are selected. Suppose you bet on 2 and 9. What is the probability that
    a) you match both numbers?   b) you match neither number?

    c) you match at least one number?

11) Two letters are chosen at random from the word CROQUET. What is the probability that both are vowels?

12) Suppose you are dealt three cards from a regular deck of cards. What is the probability that all three will be jacks?

13) In a Win, Lose, or Draw class, five of the twelve females are blonde and six of the fifteen males are blondes. What is the probability of selecting a female or a blonde?

14) You roll a fair die four times. What is the probability that you roll at least one 6?

15) You have played soccer for many seasons and have stored all of the leftover socks in a drawer. You've lost a few, so now you have 4 red, 5 green, and 7 blue socks. If you reach in and grab 2 socks at random, what is the probability:
   a) both are red?   b) both are green?

   c) both are blue?   d) neither is red?

   e) at least one is red?   f) the socks don't match?

16) You and a friend each pick a card from a regular deck of cards but do not look at them. Both of you then hold your cards up by your foreheads so that you can see each other's card but you can't see your own. Your friend is holding a 6. What is the probability that your card is higher (assume Aces are high)?

17) To win the jackpot of a state lottery game, you must correctly pick the six numbers selected from the given numbers (order doesn't matter). What is the probability of winning the state lottery in the following states:
   a) Massachusetts #'s 1 through 36   b) New York #'s 1 through 40

18) You flip a coin 7 times in a row. What is the probability of getting:
   a) 2 tails?   b) 5 heads?

   c) at most 2 tails?   d) at least one tail?

19) There are 15 first years, 7 sophomores, and 3 juniors in a class. A group of 6 is to be formed to make a presentation at a conference. Find the following.

    a) P(all first years)   b) P(no sophomores)

    c) P(2 first years)   d) P(3 sophomores)

    e) P(at least 5 first years)   f) P(at least 1 sophomore)

20) Two cards are drawn at the same time from a standard deck. What's the probability of getting:

    a) both aces or both face cards?   b) both black or both face cards?

    c) both aces or both black?   d) both are aces or both are jacks?

21) What is the probability of being issued a 10 digit Indiana driver's license number which has:

    a) no 7's?   b) five 7's?

    c) five 7's and no 6's?   d) five 7's and three 6's?

    e) five 7's, three 6's, and no 8's or 9's?

GROUP #15

The Monty Hall Problem
Let's Make a Deal

Door #1   Door #2   Door #3

The game show *Let's Make a Deal* which is now hosted by Wayne Brady, used to be hosted by Monty Hall when it started in 1963. The idea is simple; a contestant would be given the choice of whatever was behind either Door #1, #2, or #3. Two of the doors had a goat (or nothing) behind them and the other door had a car (or some other nice prize). The contestant was asked to choose one of the doors. Once the contestant had chosen, at least one of the remaining doors had a goat behind it. Monty would then open a remaining door with the goat behind it and offer the contestant a chance to switch doors with the other remaining door.

THE MONTY HALL PROBLEM: Is it better for the contestant to stay or switch?

In order to answer this question, we will have each group member do a series of trials acting as contestants; staying and switching on subsequent turns.

15.1) Before we do any trials what do you think: is it better for the contestant to stay, switch, or it doesn't make a difference?

15.2) Take 3 cards from your deck- one black (acting as the car) and two red (acting as the goats). Each member of your group will act as the contestant ten times.

    a) Place the three cards face down in a row after shuffling them.

    b) Choose one of the cards.

    d) First 5 times for each contestant, **stay**. Turn your card over. If it's a black, you would keep it and win! If it's a red, you would keep it and lose. Record if you won (got black) or lost (got a red) when you stayed.

    e) Last 5 times for each contestant, **switch**. Turn over your card. If it's a black, you would switch to a red and lose. If it's a red, you would switch to the black and win! Record if you won (got black) or lost (got a red) when you switched.

	WON		LOST	
	your own trials	group total	your own trials	group total
STAY				
SWITCH				

15.3) After seeing your group totals, do you think you should stay or switch?

74

15.4) Now we'll look at the actual probabilities to get a theoretical answer. If you choose the door with the car behind it for your initial choice, it's better to stay. What's the probability that you choose the car right off the bat?

15.5) If you chose a door with a goat behind it for your initial choice, it's better to switch. What is the probability that you choose one of the goats with your initial choice?

15.6) So what does it look like would be better to do, stay or switch? Explain.

15.7) We'll draw a tree now to better illustrate this. It is called a decision tree, and each bud produces branches whose probabilities must add up to 1. We assume **THE CONTESTANT CHOOSES DOOR #1**.

    1) Add a probability to each tree branch.

    2) Add the door number for each door the host could show in each situation.

    3) Fill in the total probability by multiplying the branches.

    4) Say what you would get if you either stay or switch from your first pick of Door #1.

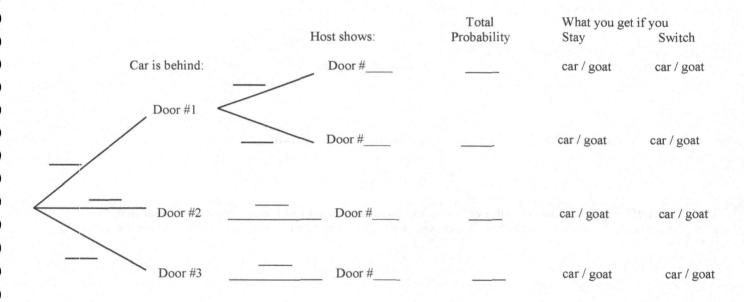

15.8) From this tree, what is the probability of getting

a) a goat if you switch?   b) a car if you stay?   c) a goat if you stay?   d) a car if you switch?

15.9) State in your own words how you would explain why you should switch to someone else.

15.10) What changes if there are four doors (one with a car and 3 with a goat), and you get to see what is behind two of them after you make your initial choice of door? Draw a tree assuming **THE CONTESTANT CHOOSES DOOR #1** and determine the probability of winning if you switch and if you stay.

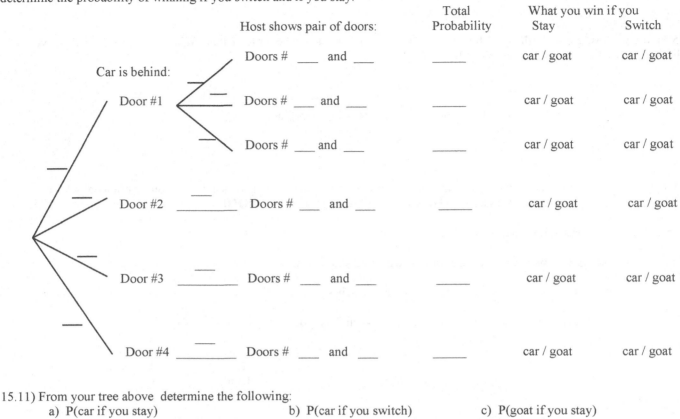

	Host shows pair of doors:	Total Probability	What you win if you	
			Stay	Switch
Car is behind: Door #1	Doors # ___ and ___	____	car / goat	car / goat
	Doors # ___ and ___	____	car / goat	car / goat
	Doors # ___ and ___	____	car / goat	car / goat
Door #2 ____	Doors # ___ and ___	____	car / goat	car / goat
Door #3 ____	Doors # ___ and ___	____	car / goat	car / goat
Door #4 ____	Doors # ___ and ___	____	car / goat	car / goat

15.11) From your tree above determine the following:
   a) P(car if you stay)   b) P(car if you switch)   c) P(goat if you stay)

   d) P(goat if you switch)   e) Should you stay or switch?

15.12) What if there were 5 doors (1 with a car and 4 with goats) and the host will open 3 of them to reveal goats?
a) P(goat if you stay)   b) P(car if you switch)   c) P(car if you stay)   d) P(goat if you switch)

15.13) What if there were 10 doors (1 with a car and 9 with goats) and the host will open 8 of them to reveal goats?
a) P(goat if you switch)   b) P(car if you stay)   c) P(car if you switch)   d) P(goat if you stay)

15.14) What if there are N doors (1 with a car and N – 1 with goats) and the host will open N – 2 of them to reveal goats?
   a) P(car if you stay)   b) P(car if you switch)   c) P(goat if you switch)

   d) P(goat if you stay)   e) Should you stay or switch?

Odds & Probability Problems

Convert the given probabilities into odds in favor of E happening.

15.15)   a) $P(E) = \frac{4}{5}$
b) $P(E) = \frac{1}{8}$
c) $P(E) = 0.28$

Odds = _____
Odds = _____
Odds = _____

Convert the given probabilities into odds of E NOT happening.

15.16)   a) $P(E) = \frac{3}{17}$
b) $P(E) = \frac{11}{40}$
c) $P(E) = 0.8$

Odds against = _____
Odds against = _____
Odds against = _____

Convert the given odds in favor of E occurring to probabilities (leave in fraction form).

15.17)   a) 5:11
b)   3:2
c)   9:5

P(E) = _____
P(E) = _____
P(E) = _____

Convert the given odds against E occurring to probabilities (leave in fraction form).

15.18)   a) 4:5
b)   9:1
c) 2:9

P(E) = _____
P(E) = _____
P(E) = _____

15.19) If a card is drawn at random from a standard deck of cards, what are the odds against the card being an ace?

15.20) A survey conducted by the U.S. Bureau of the Census in 1997 showed that 84% of the people in the United States are covered by health insurance. What are the odds a person in the United States is covered by health insurance?

15.21) The odds against winning a $2 prize in the Lucky Gold game from the Colorado Lottery are 9:2. What is the probability of winning $2 in the game?

15.22) If a game spinner has a 3/8 probability of landing on blue, what are the odds of the spinner landing on blue?

15.23) In the game of Monopoly, players roll two dice and move the number of spaces as indicated by the sum of the two dice. Pennsylvania Avenue is five spaces from Boardwalk on the game board. What are the odds that a player on Pennsylvania Avenue will land on Boardwalk by rolling the dice? Hint: there are 36 different possible outcomes when rolling two dice.

GROUP #16

Slot Machines

Questions are taken from
The Slot Machine Answer Book 2nd ed. 2005 by John Grochowski
See how many of the following you can get right!

1) In the US, slot machines account for:
   a) about 40% of casino revenue
   b) about 50% of casino revenue
   c) about 60% of casino revenue
   d) more than 70% of casino revenue

2) The number of slot machines in use in the US (as of 2017) is:
   a) about 300,000
   b) about 500,000
   c) about 700,000
   d) more than 900,000

3) The most common coins played in US slot machines are worth:
   a) 1 cent
   b) 5 cents
   c) 25 cents
   d) $1

4) Outside of Nevada the state with the most slot machines is:
   a) New Jersey
   b) Mississippi
   c) California
   d) Oklahoma

5) The largest slot jackpot ever hit in the US is:
   a) $9.7 million
   b) $19.7 million
   c) $29.7 million
   d) $39.7 million

6) Playing more than one machine at a time:
   a) narrows the house edge.
   b) ensures the player of finding at least one loose machine.
   c) costs the player more money in the long run.

7) Instead of cash, early slot machines sometimes paid:
   a) golf balls
   b) chewing gum
   c) cigars
   d) all of the above

8) Orange, plum, and lemon symbols, all still used on slot machines today, were introduced on slot machine to signify:
   a) the inventor's roots as a fruit-stand vendor.
   b) flavors of chewing gum.
   c) wealth, as fresh fruit then was so expensive.
   d) none of the above.

9) The device with inner working most like a modern slot machine is:
   a) a 1960s slot machine
   b) a coin-operated gumball machine
   c) an electric clock
   d) a personal computer

10) The probabilty of winning on an old-style mechanical slot machine are determined by:
   a) the number of symbols and spaces on each reel.
   b) the number of reels.
   c) both of the above.
   d) none of the above.

11) The probability of winning on an modern slot machine are determined by:
   a) the number of symbols and spaces on each reel.
   b) the number of reels.
   c) both of the above.
   d) none of the above.

12) A machine is programmed to pay a jackpot about once per 10,000 pulls. You have played 9,999 pulls without hitting a jackpot. The probability of hitting on the next pull are:
   a) even
   b) 1 in 100
   c) 1 in 10,000
   d) undetermined

13) A machine is programmed to pay a jackpot about once per 10,000 pulls. You just won a jackpot on your last pull. The probability of hitting again on next pull are:
   a) 1 in 10,000
   b) 1 in 100,000
   c) 1 in 1 million
   d) undetermined

14) After playing a slot machine for 2 hours, you walk away. The player who replaces you immediately hits the jackpot. If you had stayed:
   a) You would have hit the jackpot.
   b) You would have had about a 50% chance of hitting the jackpot.
   c) Your chances of hitting the jackpot would have been very small.

15) Slot players increase their chances of winning by playing:
   a) Slots on which they have seen others winning.
   b) Slots on which they have seen others losing.
   c) Slots that haven't been played in a few hours.
   d) none of the above.

Example: A slot machine has 3 reels each with 9 symbols (including 1 jackpot on each reel).
   a) How many different results would occur with one spin?

   b) P(3 jackpots)   c) P(2 jackpots)

   d) P(1 jackpot)   e) P(0 jackpots)

   f) Suppose that there are still 3 reels each with 9 symbols, but now there 4 jackpots on each reel.
      i) P(3 jackpots)   ii) P(1 jackpot)

16.1) A slot machine has 4 reels and each reel has 8 different symbols (each including one jackpot).
   a) How many different results could occur in one spin?

   b) What is the probability of getting all 4 jackpots?   c) What is the probability of getting no jackpots?

   d) What is the probability of getting 1 jackpot?   e) What is the probability of getting 2 jackpots?

16.2) Another slot machine has 8 reels each with 4 different symbols, each including one jackpot.
   a) How many different results could occur in one spin?

   b) P(8 jackpots)   c) P(no jackpots)

16.3) A slot machine has 3 reels each with 10 symbols. There is one jackpot symbol on each reel.
   a) How many different results could occur in one spin?

   b) What is the probability of getting:
      i) all three jackpots?   ii) exactly 2 jackpots?

      iii) at least 2 jackpots?   iv) no jackpots?

16.4) A slot machine named Big Blue has 4 reels each with 11 different symbols. There is one bulldog on each reel.
   a) How many different results could occur in one spin?

   b) P(no bulldogs)   c) P(3 bulldogs)

   d) P(at least 1 bulldog)   e) P(at least 3 bulldogs)

16.5) A slot machine has 5 reels each with 7 different symbols (including one jackpot on each reel).
   a) How many different results could occur in one spin?

   b) P(no jackpots)   c) P(1 jackpot)

   d) P(2 jackpots)   e) P(3 jackpots)

   f) P(4 jackpots)   g) P(5 jackpots)

16.6) A slot machine has 4 reels each with 15 symbols including THREE jackpots on each reel.
   a) How many different results could occur in one spin?

   b) P(4 jackpots)   c) P(no jackpots)

   d) P(1 jackpot)   e) P(2 jackpots)

   f) P(3 jackpots)   g) P(at least 1 jackpot)

16.7)   Jokers Wild is a slot machine that has 3 reels each with 20 symbols. Its first reel has 4 joker symbols; second has 3 joker symbols; and third has 2 joker symbols.
   a) How many different results could occur in one spin?

   b) P(3 jokers)   c) P(no jokers)

   d) P(at least 1 joker)   e) P(2 jokers)

   f) P(1 joker)   g) P(at most 1 joker)

16.8) A slot machine has 3 reels each with 10 symbols consisting of 6 lemons, 3 cherries, and 1 bell.
   a) How many different results could occur in one spin?

   b) P(3 lemons)   c) P(no cherries)

   d) P(at least 1 cherries)   e) P(3 different symbols)

16.9) You roll a die 7 times in a row.
   a) How many different results could occur?

   b) P(no 4s)   c) P(one 2)

   d) P(three 1s)   e) P(four 6s)

81

GROUP #17

Dice Games: Risk and Craps

There are many, many games which require you to roll dice in order to play. In this group we will focus on Risk and Craps. First we will look at rolling a pair of dice and how many different outcomes there could be.

With perfectly balanced dice, each combination on a pair of dice is equally likely. The table below shows all of the possible outcomes for rolling a pair of dice (upper left number is die #1 and lower right number is die #2). You can think of them as 2 different colors so that you can tell them apart.

1 1	1 2	1 3	1 4	1 5	1 6
2 1	2 2	2 3	2 4	2 5	2 6
3 1	3 2	3 3	3 4	3 5	3 6
4 1	4 2	4 3	4 4	4 5	4 6
5 1	5 2	5 3	5 4	5 5	5 6
6 1	6 2	6 3	6 4	6 5	6 6

17.1) How many total outcomes are there?

17.2) From the above table, knowing all outcomes are equally likely, determine the following:

a) P(doubles)   b) P(sum of 2)   c) P(sum of 3)

d) P(sum of 4)   e) P(sum of 5)   f) P(sum of 6)

g) P(sum of 7)   h) P(sum of 8)   i) P(sum of 9)

j) P(sum of 10)   k) P(sum of 11)   l) P(sum of 12)

m) P(sum of 3 or 10)   n) P(sum of at least 9)   o) P(sum of at most 5)

RISK In the game of Risk, the board is just a map of the world with continents sectioned off. You and your opponent place armies on different territories and then attack each other to try to attain more territories (the goal is world domination).

- When an attack is made, **the attacker gets to roll three dice and the defender only rolls two**.
- The attacker's highest die number is compared to the defender's highest die.
- The attacker's next highest die is compared against the defender's second highest die. The attacker's lowest die does not count.
- **The defender wins in the case of a tie**.
- With each dice comparison, the loser removes one army from his territory on the game board. So there are three things that can happen in an attack:

     1)   the attacker loses 2 armies
     2)   the defender loses 2 armies
     3)   they split and each loses one army

Example of each: 1) Attacker rolls 6, 3, 3 and defender rolls 6, 4, then the attacker will lose two armies.
    2) Attacker rolls 4, 5, 2 and defenders rolls 3, 4, then the defender will lose two armies.
    3) Attacker rolls 1, 2, 5 and defender rolls 5, 1, then they both lose one army.

PLAY MINI GAME OF RISK With the given dice, play this mini game of Risk with your group. Each side of the table starts with 10 pennies (armies). Take turns being the attacker and defender and lose your pennies according to the rules above.

Game 1 results: Who won? _____ Defender _____ Attacker

Game 2 results: Who won? _____ Defender _____ Attacker

For the following problems, a scenario is given with one or two of the dice rolls unknown. You are to determine probabilities of each type of result by first listing the outcomes for each category and then determine their probabilities.
    Here's an example:

Ex. Attacker: 5, 3, ?   Defender: 5, 4
a) P(attacker loses 2 armies)   b) P(defender loses 2 armies)   c) P(both lose one army)

17.3) Attacker: 3, 6, 2   Defender: 4, ?
  a) P(attacker loses 2 armies)   b) P(defender loses 2 armies)   c) P(both lose one army)

17.4) Attacker: 6, 2, ?   Defender: 2, 3
  a) P(attacker loses 2 armies)   b) P(defender loses 2 armies)   c) P(both lose one army)

17.5) Attacker: 3, 1, ?   Defender: 1, 3
  a) P(attacker loses 2 armies)   b) P(defender loses 2 armies)   c) P(both lose one army)

THE GAME OF CRAPS (for a PASS LINE BET)

1. Roll a pair of dice.
      *Sum of 7 or 11 (**natural**), you win an even money payout*
            (for a $1 bet, you'll get $1 plus keep your bet)
      *Sum of 2, 3, or 12 (**craps**), you lose your bet*
      *Sum of 4, 5, 6, 8, 9, or 10 is called your **point**.*

2. If you roll a point on your first roll, then you continue to roll the dice.
      If you roll your point again before rolling a 7 then you win an even money payout.
      If you roll a 7 before you roll your point again, you lose your bet.

17.6) a) What is the probability that you roll a natural on your first roll? i.e. P(sum of 7 or 11)

b) What is the probability that you "crap out" on your first roll? i.e. P(sum of 2, 3, or 12)

c) What is the probability that you get a point on your first roll? i.e. P(sum of 4, 5, 6, 8, 9, or 10)

d) After you roll a point on your 1st roll, what is the probability you roll a sum 7 on the 2nd roll and lose?

e) After you roll a point on your first roll, what is the probability that you don't roll a 7 on the 2nd roll?

f) After you roll a point on your 1st roll and neither a sum of 7 or your point on the second roll, what is the probability that you roll a 7 on your 3rd roll? Did this probability change at all from d) and e)? Why or why not?

17.7) If two dice are rolled, what is the probability that:
  a) you don't roll doubles?   b) the sum is odd?   c) the sum is 7 or 8?

  d) the sum is not 7 nor 8?   e) the sum is at least 7?   f) the sum is at most 6?

  g) two 3's?   h) one 3?   i) no 3's?

17.8) If you were to roll a pair of dice, what would be your best guess for the sum? Why?

17.9) Attacker: 4, 1, 6   Defender: 2, ?
   a) P(attacker loses 2 armies)   b) P(defender loses 2 armies)   c) P(both lose one army)

17.10) Attacker: 3, 2, ?   Defender: 4, 2
   a) P(attacker loses 2 armies)   b) P(defender loses 2 armies)   c) P(both lose one army)

17.11) Attacker: 3, 3, 3   Defender: 3, ?
   a) P(attacker loses 2 armies)   b) P(defender loses 2 armies)   c) P(both lose one army)

17.12) Let's say you are the attacker and roll 3 dice.
   a) How many different outcomes are there?   b) P(triples)

   c) P(three 6's)   d) P(no 6's)   e) P(at least one 6)

   f) P(two 6's)   g) P(one 6)

17.13) Some games actually use 20 sided dice. Say you roll a pair of 20 sided dice.
   a) How many different outcomes are there?   b) What different sums are possible?

   c) P(doubles)   d) P(sum of 2)   e) P(sum of 8)

MORE PROBABILITY NOTES

CONDITIONAL PROBABILITY

P(rolling a 5) =   , but what if we know that we rolled an odd number?

P(rolling a 5 | rolled odd) =   P(rolling a 5 | rolled even) =

$$P(B \mid A) = \frac{P(A \cap B)}{P(A)}$$ "the probability of B given A"

(given that event A occurred, we determine the probability of B occurring)

Ex1. Using the formula, find P(rolling a 5 | rolled odd)

Ex2. A card is drawn from a deck.
a) P(spade | not red)   b) P(red | not a spade)   c) P(face | spade or jack)

Ex3. Out of 100 students, 50 play soccer, 70 play basketball, and 40 play both. Find the probability that a student chosen at random plays:
a) neither sport.   b) basketball but not soccer.   c) soccer given they play basketball.

d) basketball given they don't play soccer.   e) doesn't play soccer given they don't play basketball.

Ex4. Two cards are randomly drawn from a deck of cards.
a) P(both are face cards)   b) P(both are kings | both are face cards)

c) P(both are hearts | both are red)   d) P(both are face cards | both are red)

INDEPENDENT 2 events A and B are independent if A doesn't affect B

$$P(B \mid A) = P(B) \quad \text{or} \quad P(A \cap B) = P(A) \cdot P(B)$$

Examples: flipping a coin multiple times, rolling a die multiple times, etc.

Ex 1. One card is drawn from a deck and then a second card is drawn. Find the probability that both of the cards are face cards if the cards are drawn:
      a) with replacement.   b) without replacement

Ex 2. At a wrestling match you buy a bag of M&M's. The bag contains the following colors: 12 red, 12 blue, 7 green, 13 brown, 3 orange, and 10 yellow, you grab 3 candies from the 57 M&M's in the bag.
      a) Find the probability of getting 2 browns and 1 orange.

      b) If you grab the candies one at a time without replacement, find the probability that 1st is brown, 2nd is orange, and 3rd is another brown.

HOMEWORK PROBLEMS:

1) If you were to spin the wheel, it is equally likely to stop at any point. Find the probability of spinning

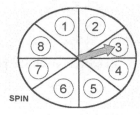

    a) a 5   b) an even number   c) at least a 3

    d) at most a 3   e) any number but 6   f) a 7 on 1st spin and an 8 on 2nd spin

    g) 4 given that you spun an even   h) a 5 or 6 given that you spun at least a 4

    i) 4 given that you spun an odd   j) odd given that you spun at most a 5

2) A pair of dice (one green, the other red) is rolled and the sum is noted. Find the following probabilities.
   a) P(doubles | sum is 8)   b) P(one die is a 6 | sum is 7)

   c) P(sum is 8 | doubles)   d) P(doubles | sum at least 9)

3) Here is a breakdown of the U.S. Senate in the 114th Congress as of September of 2015:

	Democrats (D)	Republicans (R)	Independents (I)	Totals
Male (M)	30	48	2	80
Female (F)	14	6	0	20
Totals	44	54	2	100

   a) Find the probability that a senator is female given they are Republican.

   b) P(F | D)   c) P(D | F)   d) P(R | F)

   e) P(I | F)   f) P(R or D | M)   g) P(M | I^C)

4) Out of 250 third-grade girls, 120 played volleyball, 140 played soccer, and 50 played both. Find the probability that a girl chosen at random played:
   a) neither sport   b) exactly one sport   c) soccer, but not volleyball

   d) soccer, given she played volleyball   e) volleyball, given she didn't play soccer

   f) didn't play soccer, given she didn't play volleyball

5) A card is drawn from a standard deck.
   a) P(queen | face card)   b) P(2 | face card)   c) P(face card | not a 10)

   d) P(8 | not a face card)   e) P(ace | neither red nor a face card)

6) There are 25 students in a class with 15 females and 10 males. Three students are needed to represent the class in a county wide competition.

    a) What is the probability that 2 females and 1 male are chosen?

    b) If the three students are chosen one at a time, what is the probability that the first is a female, the second is a male, and the third is another female?

7) Of 100 athletes, 30 wrestle, 25 play hockey, 40 play softball, 6 wrestle and play hockey, 8 play hockey and softball, 5 play softball and wrestle but not hockey, and 4 play all three sports.

    a) P(wrestle | play softball)

    b) P(play both hockey and softball | wrestle)

    c) P(don't play softball or wrestle | don't play hockey)

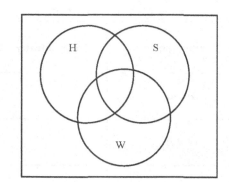

8) A penny is flipped 4 times. Determine the following conditional probabilities.

    a) P(3 heads | at least 1 head)   b) P(exactly 2 tails | at least 2 tails)

9) Three cards are drawn from a deck.

    a) P(all are clubs | all are black)   b) P(all are face cards | all are black)

    c) P(all are aces | no faces cards)   d) P(at least 2 spades | no hearts)

10) When rolling 5 dice, what is the probability of rolling all 6's given that you rolled at least four 6's?

GROUP #18

Roulette:
What Are the Odds?

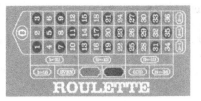

Roulette is the oldest casino game still being played. The American roulette wheel has 38 numbered compartments, the numbers 1 through 36, plus 0 and 00 (**which are not considered even**). Players place bets by putting their chips on the appropriate spot on the roulette table (shown). Then the dealer spins the wheel and drops a ball onto the spinning wheel; once the ball starts its descent (starts dropping to the numbers), the dealer calls "No more bets". When the ball finally stops, that compartment it lands in is the winning number. At this point the dealer places a marker on the winning number, sweeps all of the losing bets off the layout, and then pays the winning bets starting with the "outside" bets (left and side of table on next page) and finishes with the "inside" bets (right side on the numbers). The dealer pays them according to the House Odds which we will compare to the true odds.

18.1) Fill in the table with the probabilities of each bet and then their true odds (usually given as against winning).

What you bet on	Probability	True Odds Against Winning		House Odds
		b to a	**c to 1** (go 2 decimal places)	
single # (*plain*)				35 to 1
two #'s (*split*)				17 to 1
three #'s (*street*)				11 to 1
four #'s (*corner*)				8 to 1
five #'s (*5-bet*)				6 to 1
six #'s (*line*)				5 to 1
twelve #'s (*column* or *dozen*)				2 to 1
low 1 to 18 (or *high* 19 to 36)				1 to 1
even (or odd)				1 to 1
red (or black)				1 to 1

18.2) Why do you suppose casinos use House Odds instead of True Odds?

18.3) We will now compare the payoffs for certain bets using the actual odds and the house odds. Let's say that you place a **$10 chip** on the following areas of the table (in other words you make a $10 bet).

If you win $10 bet on the following, how much would you win (plus you get to keep your bet on the table)?

a) **13b**   True odds payout _____

House odds payout _____

b) **2b, 5r**   True odds payout _____

House odds payout _____

c) **19r, 20b, 21r** True odds payout _____

House odd payout _____

d) **28b, 29b, 31b, 32r** True odds payout _____

House odds payout _____

e) **0, 00, 1r, 2b, 3r** True odds payout _____

House odds payout _____

f) **13b,14r, 15b,16r, 17b,18r** True odds payout _____

House odds payout _____

g) **1ˢᵗ 12**   True odds payout _____

House odds payout _____

h) **black**   True odds payout _____

House odds payout _____

		0	00	
1 to 18		1 red	2 black	3 red
		4 black	5 red	6 black
	1ˢᵗ 12	7 red	8 black	9 red
Even		10 black	11 black	12 red
		13 black	14 red	15 black
Red		16 red	17 black	18 red
	2ⁿᵈ 12	19 red	20 black	21 red
Black		22 black	23 red	24 black
		25 red	26 black	27 red
Odd		28 black	29 black	30 red
	3ʳᵈ 12	31 black	32 red	33 black
19 to 36		34 red	35 black	36 red

PLAY ROULETTE Now we'll all play roulette and make bets. Using one of the roulette tables for your group, everyone in the group place a bet where you want to make a bet.

The wheel will be spun and those who win, get the house odds pay out plus they get to keep their bet. Those who lose, lose their bet.

To place bets on something that is not just one square (a single #, 1 to 18, even, red, 1st 12, etc):

For a 2 # split, place the bet on the line between the two numbers.
For a 3 # street, place the bet at the end of the three number line.
For a 4 # corner, place the bet in the middle of the square of 4 numbers.
For a 5 # bet, it has to be for 0, 00, 1r, 2b, 3r and is placed at the end of the intersection of the top two lines.
For a 6 # bet, place the bet at the end of the two three number lines at their intersection.
For a 12 # column bet, place the bet at the bottom of the column.
For all other bets, just place your bet in the marked box.

Keep track of your money after each bet:

Start with $ 40   after 1st round _____   after 2nd rd _____   after 3rd rd _____   after 4th rd _____

18.4) For further problems, we'll focus on conditional probability. Let's assume the ball has already landed on a number, but the spinner is covered. Find the following conditional probabilities that the winning number is:

a) P(4 given that its black)

b) P(12 or 14 | even)

c) P(odd given that it's in 2nd 12)

d) P(red | 19 to 36)

e) P(at least 30 given that it's in 3rd 12)

f) P(19 | odd)

g) P(at most 10 given it's black)

h) P(36 | black)

i) P(red given it's 27)

j) P(even | 20)

k) P(in 1st 12 given it's odd)

l) P(black | at least 28)

m) P(in 19 to 36 given that it's divisible by 5)

n) P(3rd 12 | at most 13)

		0		00
1 to 18	1st 12	1 r	2 b	3 r
		4 b	5 r	6 b
		7 r	8 b	9 r
Even		10 b	11 b	12 r
Red	2nd 12	13 b	14 r	15 b
		16 r	17 b	18 r
		19 r	20 b	21 r
Black		22 b	23 r	24 b
Odd	3rd 12	25 r	26 b	27 r
		28 b	29 b	30 r
		31 b	32 r	33 b
19 to 36		34 r	35 b	36 r

18.5) You place a $20 bet on a street (3 numbers) and the house odds are 11 to 1.
   a) What is the probability that you will win?

   b) What are the odds against you winning your bet?

   c) How much would the casino give you if you win your bet (don't include your bet that gets to stay on the table)?

18.6) You place a $50 bet on the middle column (twelve numbers) and the house odds are 2 to 1.
   a) What is the probability that you will lose your bet?

   b) What are the odds of winning your bet?

   c) What would your payout be if you win your bet (not including your bet that stays on the table)?

Review problems:
18.7) A slot machine has 4 reels each with 20 symbols (including 2 jackpots on each).
   a) How many different outcomes are there?

   b) P(no jackpots)   c) P(4 jackpots)

   d) P(3 jackpots)   e) P(at least one jackpot)

18.8) Two cards are drawn from a deck of cards.
   a) P(exactly 1 king | both are face)   b) P(both are face | exactly 1 king)

GROUP #19

Bayes Theorem

Bayes Theorem goes hand in hand with conditional probability. Before we see the actual theorem, we will look at an example about prenatal genetic testing for Down Syndrome to understand what motivates Bayes Theorem.

Ex. Pregnant women get a first trimester screening which is used to detect Down Syndrome (Trisomy 21 and 18). The screening will detect the presence of the birth defect 85% of the time. It is believed that 5% of pregnant women where Down Syndrome is NOT present are told they tested positive by the screening. (This is known as a FALSE POSITIVE.)

a) Down Syndrome occurs in about 1 in 1300 pregnancies of a 25 year old woman. If the screening positively detected the presence of the birth defect in a 25 year old pregnant woman, what is the probability that Down Syndrome is actually present? Let DS = has Down Syndrome.

- First determine what the question is asking us.

$$\text{Find P(} \quad | \quad)$$

- Next we will determine the following: P(DS) = _____   P(not DS) = _____   P(tests + |DS) = _____

  P(tests − | DS) = _____   P(tests + | not DS) = _____   P(tests − | not DS) = _____

- Make a probability tree.

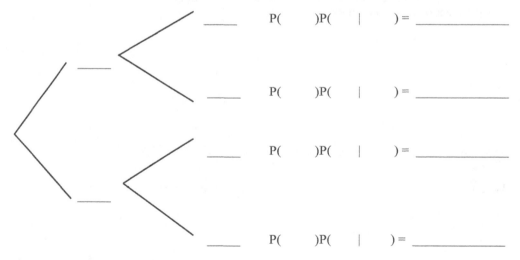

- Now we can determine our answer.

b) For a 45 year old woman the risk goes up to 1 in 35. Determine P(DS | +) for a 45 year old woman.

Bayes Theorem is a fancy way of saying what we just determined using the probability tree. Here is the short form:

BAYES THEOREM $$P(B \mid A) = \frac{P(A \mid B)P(B)}{P(A)} = \frac{P(A \mid B)P(B)}{P(A \mid B)P(B) + P(A \mid B^C)P(B^C)}$$

19.1) A manufacturer claims that their test will detect steroid use (i.e. positive result for an athlete who uses steroids) 95% of the time. What the manufacturer does not tell you is that 10% of those who do not use steroids test positive (known as a FALSE POSITIVE). On the rugby team, 20% of the athletes use steroids. What is the probability a player on the rugby team who tests negative doesn't use steroids? U = uses, DU = doesn't use.

What are we looking for?   P(|)

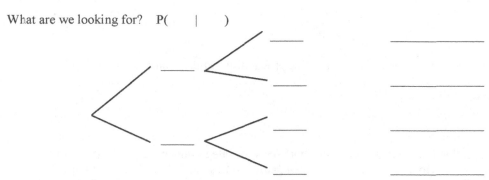

Determine the answer.

19.2) A test for a genetic disorder can detect with 94% accuracy. The test will incorrectly report positive results for 3% of those individuals without the disorder (a false positive). If 12% of the population has the disorder, find the probability that someone who tests positive has the disorder.

What are you looking for?   P(|)

19.3) A fictional casino has two types of slot machines, type A which hit a jackpot 1% of the time and type B that hit a jackpot 10% of the time. Of the casino's 100 slot machines, only 2 of them are type B. If someone hits the jackpot, what is the probability that they were at a type B slot machine?

What are you looking for?   P(|)

19.4) Holmes Sports Outlet receives 70% of its track spikes from LA and 30% from NY. The spikes from NY are defective 10% of the time, and those from LA are defective 5% of the time.
    a) If a randomly selected pair of spikes is found to be defective, what is the probability that they came from NY?

        What are you looking for? P(|)

    b) If it is known that a pair of spikes is not defective, what is the probability that they came from NY?

        What are you looking for? P(|)

19.5) As winter approaches many college students will get a flu shot. 65% of college students get a flu shot. Of the students getting a flu shot, 15% will contract a flu virus. Of those students *not* getting a flu shot, 72% will contract a flu virus.
    a) A college student with the flu virus is selected at random, what is the probability that the student had a flu shot?

        What are you looking for? P(|)

    b) What is the probability that a student who did not get the flu, did not have a flu shot?

        What are you looking for? P(|)

19.6) A biker is doing a ride with a group of friends but gets lost. There are 3 roads at the next intersection. If the biker selects road A, the probability they will find their friends is 1/4. If they select road B, the probability is 1/5, and if they select road C, the probability is 1/6. The probability that the biker chooses any of these roads is the same. If the biker does find his friends, what is the probability that they travelled on road B?

        What are you looking for? P(|)

19.7) It is estimated that the NCAA rents 53% of their cars from Agency A, 16% from Agency B, and 31% from Agency C. It is also estimated that 27% of cars from A need a tune up, 12% from B, and 22% from C. If a rental car delivered to the NCAA needs a tune up, what is the probability that it came from:

   a) A?

   b) B?

   c) C?

Review Problems:
19.8) You roll a pair of dice (one green, one red).
   a) P(roll a sum of 10)   b) P(don't roll doubles | sum of 10)

19.9) Monty Hall has invited you on to his show Lets Make a Deal and shows you 7 doors (one with a car behind it and 6 with goats). He asks you to choose a door and then opens 5 of the other doors to reveal 5 goats. Then he asks if you want to stay with your original or switch to the other door.
   a) P(car if you stay)   b) P(goat if you stay)   c) P(car if you switch)

   d) P(goat if you switch)   e) Should you stay or switch?

19.10) You place a $25 bet on a line (6 numbers) and the house odds are 5 to 1.
   a) What is the probability that you will win?

   b) What are the odds against you winning your bet?

   c) How much would the casino give you if you win your bet (don't include your bet that gets to stay on the table)?

Poker Hands

There are 10 different types of poker hands, and you will need to know them so that we can determine their probabilities next group. For this group we will learn what they are, how they are ranked, and then find probabilities of other 5 card hands.

20.1) Here is a list of each type of poker hand. Rank the types in order from 1 to 10, 1 being the most probable hand (lowest ranked hand; every other hand beats it) and 10 being the least probable hand (highest ranked hand; beats every other hand).

_____**Flush**: consists of 5 cards of the same suit but are not consecutive ranks
        ex. {4♠, 7♠, 10♠, Q♠, K♠}

_____**One Pair**: consists of 2 cards of one rank, and 3 singletons each of a differing rank
        ex. {J♦, J♠, A♥, 4♣, 6♦}

_____**High Card Only**: consists of cards which fall in no other category, thus there are 5 different nonconsecutive
        ranks in at least 2 different suits
        ex. { A♣, 5♥, 7♥, 8♠, J♠}

_____**Royal Straight Flush**: consists of 10, J, Q, K, A of the same suit
        ex. {10♣, J♣, Q♣,, K♣, A♣}

_____**Four of a Kind**: consists of 4 cards of the same rank and one singleton
        ex. {8♥, 8♦, 8♠, 8♣, 3♥}

_____**Full House**: consists of 3 cards of the same rank and a pair of cards of another rank
        ex. {5♥, 5♠, 5♣, 9♣, 9♦}

_____**Two Pair**: consists of 2 cards of one rank, 2 cards of another rank, and a singleton at a third different rank
        ex. {2♥, 2♦, 6♣, 6♥, 9♦}

_____**Straight**: consists of 5 cards with consecutive ranks not all of the same suit
        ex. {6♥, 7♠, 8♦, 9♥, 10♦}

_____**Straight Flush**: consists of 5 cards with consecutive ranks in the same suit (not Royal)
        ex. {3♥, 4♥, 5♥, 6♥, 7♥}

_____**Three of a Kind**: consists of 3 cards of the same rank along with two singletons each of a differing rank
        ex. {A♣, A♦, A♥, 7♥, 8♠}

20.2) Everyone take a Pokeno card and for your card determine which type of poker hand each of the following are:

1st row across: 1st column down:

2nd row across: 2nd column down:

3rd row across: 3rd column down:

4th row across: 4th column down:

5th row across: 5th column down:

diagonal from top left to bottom right: other diagonal:

20.3) Each side of your table will take a deck of cards and using all but two cards, make each of the ten types of poker hands (10 types each with 5 cards will use 50 cards and 2 will be left out).

Five cards are dealt from a regular deck of cards. Find the following probabilities.

20.4) P(all spades)

20.5) P(all red)

20.6) P(3 clubs and 2 diamonds)

20.7) P(3 eights and 2 queens)

20.8) P(exactly 3 jacks)

20.9) P(no hearts)

20.10) P(at least 4 red)

20.11) P(at most 2 clubs)

20.12) P(no face cards)

20.13) P(at least one face card)

20.14) P(contains 2 of ♥)

20.15) P(contains all 2's but no face cards)

20.16) P(reds or 8's but no face cards)

20.17) P(jacks or clubs but no 7's)

20.18) P(all spades | all black)

20.19) P(all face cards | all red)

20.20) P(exactly 3 face cards | all clubs)

20.21) P(all hearts | no clubs)

20.22) P(no hearts | no clubs)

20.23) P(exactly 2 queens | no clubs)

20.24) P(contains 2 of ♥ | all red)

20.25) P(contains 2 of ♥ but no face cards | all red)

20.26) P(exactly 2 queens | all jacks or red)

20.27) P(at least 4 face cards | all jacks or red)

GROUP #21

Probabilities of Poker

This project will investigate the probabilities of all of the different types of poker hands which we discussed in Pokeno. One thing to note is that a Royal Straight Flush is also a Straight Flush, a Flush, and a Straight, but you would only consider it a Royal Straight Flush. Once you're done with the project, you will be able to fill out the following table and easily see why the poker hands are ranked as they are. Give probabilities to 4 significant figures (i.e. until you have 4 digits that aren't 0's).

Poker Hand	Number of Each Type of Hand	Probability (4 sig figs)
Royal Straight Flush		0.000001539
Straight Flush		0.00001385
Four of a Kind		0.0002401
Full House		0.001441
Flush		0.001965
Straight		0.003925
Three of a Kind		0.02113
Two Pair		0.04754
One Pair		0.4226
High Card Only		0.5012
Total		~1

21.1) How many different 5 card poker hands are there? Make sure you have this right because you'll use this number in every other problem!

21.2) A **Royal Straight Flush** consists of 10, J, Q, K, A of the same suit. Example: _____

 a) How many different Royal Straight Flushes are there?

 b) What is the probability that you are dealt a Royal Straight Flush?

21.3) A **Straight Flush** consists of 5 cards with consecutive ranks in the same suit, but not a Royal Straight Flush.

Example: _____

a) What ranks could be the low card in a Straight Flush?

b) Given your answer in a), how many different Straight Flushes are there?

c) What is the probability that you are dealt a Straight Flush?

21.4) **Four of a Kind** consists of 4 cards of the same rank together with one singleton. Example: _____

a) How many ways are there to choose the 4 cards that are of the same rank?

b) After those 4 cards have been chosen, how many ways are there to choose the singleton?

c) Given your answers to a) and b), how many different Four of a Kinds are there?

d) What is the probability of being dealt a Four of a Kind?

21.5) A **Full House** consists of 3 cards of the same rank and a pair of cards of another rank. This one is a little more involved, so we'll think about it in pieces...

a) Choose any two ranks _____ and _____.

b) Using those two ranks, write out two different Full Houses you could have.

c) How many possible Full Houses could you have using those two ranks? Remember that either rank could be the 3 of a kind or the pair.

d) How many ways are there to choose any two ranks from the 13 in a deck of cards?

e) To figure out the total number of Full Houses, think of choosing your two ranks first (your answer from d)) and from there figure out how many ways there are to arrange those ranks into Full Houses (your answer from c)). How many different Full Houses could you be dealt?

f) So what is the probability that you are dealt a Full House?

21.6) A **Flush** consists of 5 cards of the same suit. Example: _____

   a) How many different hands have 5 cards of the same suit?

   b) The answer for a) will not be the right number of Flushes though because Royal Straight Flushes and Straight Flushes have already been counted, so we'll need to subtract them from a). So how many Flushes are there?

   c) So what is the probability that you are dealt a Flush?

21.7) A **Straight** consists of 5 cards with consecutive ranks in any number of suits. Example: _____

   a) List the ranks that could be the low card in any straight (include 10 as well). So how many cards could be the low card?

   b) After you choose the low card of the straight, how many ways are there to choose each consecutive rank in any suit which will have to be done 4 times?

   c) How many hands have 5 ranks in consecutive order?

   d) We again have to subtract the Royal Straight Flushes and Straight Flushes. How many different Straights are there?

   e) And the probability of being dealt a Straight?

21.8) **Three of a Kind** consists of 3 cards of the same rank along with two singletons each of a differing rank, so 3 different ranks are needed. Try to work this one out as we did the Full House: choose the ranks first, then which of those will be the triple, and then the actual cards of each rank.

                           Example: _____
   a) How many different Three of a Kinds are there?

   b) What is the probability of being dealt a Three of a Kind?

21.9) **Two Pair** consists of 2 cards of one rank, 2 cards of another rank, and a singleton at a third rank. Again try to work this one as we did the Full House and the Three of a Kind.

Example: _____

a) How many different Two Pair are there?

b) What is the probability of being dealt Two Pair?

21.10) **One Pair** consists of 2 cards of one rank, and 3 singletons each of a differing rank, so 4 ranks are needed. Try with same method.

Example: _____

a) How many different hands have One Pair?

b) What is the probability of being dealt One Pair?

21.11) **High Card Only** When you're playing poker and no one has any of these special poker hands, the hand with the highest card (aces are high) wins and if there's a tie, you move to the 2nd high in those hands, etc. Using the table that you have filled in on the first sheet, you can figure out these answers by knowing the total number of 5 card hands and that probability adds up to 1.

a) What is the number of possible high card only hands?   Example: _____

b) What is the probability of being dealt no special poker hand and have a High Card Only hand?

21.12) Now we'll try a few 5 card poker hand problems using a deck of cards where **ALL OF THE DIAMONDS ARE REMOVED**, so there are only clubs, spades, and hearts in the deck. Notice that you cannot have a Four of a Kind now. Leave your answers as a fraction, no need to reduce and you do NOT have to subtract off Royal Straight Flush or Straight Flush.

a) How many ways are there to choose your 5 cards?

b) P(Royal Straight Flush)   Example: _____

c) P(Straight Flush)   Example: _____

d) P(Full House)   Example: _____

e) P(Flush)   Example: _____

f) P(Straight)   Example: _____

g) P(Three of a Kind)   Example: _____

h) P(Two Pair)   Example: _____

i) P(One Pair)   Example: _____

GROUP #22

Pinochle Poker

Pinochle is a game which uses a slightly different deck of cards than a standard 52 card deck. We are not going to be learning how to play pinochle but we are going to expand our version of poker using a deck of pinochle cards, so first we will need to get familiar with a pinochle deck.

22.1) Take your pinochle deck and organize the deck in suits and ranks within suits to determine the following.

a) Number of cards in a deck:

b) List the ranks in each suit:

c) Number of cards of each suit:

d) Number of cards of each rank:

e) How many face cards are there?

22.2) a) How many 5 card hands are there in pinochle poker?

b) What new types of poker hands exist when using a pinochle deck?

22.3) A **Royal Straight Flush** consists of 10, J, Q, K, A of the same suit. Example: _____
a) How many different Royal Straight Flushes are there in hearts?

b) So how many total different Royal Straight Flushes are there in pinochle poker?

c) What is the probability that you are dealt a Royal Straight Flush?

22.4) A **Straight Flush** consists of 5 cards with consecutive ranks in same suit, but not Royal. Example: _____
a) How many different Straight Flushes are there in pinochle poker?

b) What is the probability that you are dealt a Straight Flush?

106

22.5) **Five of a Kind** consists of 5 cards of the same rank.   Example: _____
a) How many different 5 of a Kind are there in pinochle poker?

b) What is the probability that you are dealt a Five of a Kind?

22.6) **Four of a Kind** consists of 4 cards of the same rank together with one singleton.   Example: _____
a) How many different Four of a Kinds are there in pinochle poker?

b) What is the probability of being dealt a Four of a Kind?

22.7) A **Flush** consists of 5 cards of the same suit. Example: _____
a) How many different hands have 5 cards of the same suit?

b) Remember the answer in a) counts the Royal and Straight Flushes, so you need to subtract to answer: How many total Flushes are there in pinochle poker?

With a pinochle deck, there are 3 types of Flushes:

- **Flush with Two Pair**
- **Flush with One Pair**
- **Flush with No Pair**

    so let's look at each of these separately…

c) Determine the number of ways and the probability of being dealt a **Flush with Two Pair** in pinochle poker.

   Example: _____

d) Determine the number of ways and the probability of being dealt a **Flush with One Pair** in pinochle poker.

        Example: _____

e) Determine the number of ways and the probability of being dealt a **Flush with No Pair** in pinochle poker. Hint: Just subtract the above two from the total number of Flushes.

        Example: _____

22.8) A **Full House** consists of 3 cards of the same rank and a pair of cards of another rank. Example: _____
   a) How many possible Full Houses are there in pinochle poker?

b) What is the probability of being dealt a Full House?

22.9) A **Straight** consists of 5 cards with consecutive ranks in any number of suits. Example: _____
   a) List the ranks that could be the low card in any straight. So how many cards could be the low card?

b) After you choose the low card of the straight, how many ways are there to choose each consecutive rank in any suit which will have to be done 4 times?

c) How many hands have 5 ranks in consecutive order?

d) We have to subtract previously counted straights. How many different Straights are there in pinochle poker?

e) And the probability of being dealt a Straight?

22.10) **Three of a Kind** consists of 3 cards of the same rank along with two singletons each of a differing rank, so 3 different ranks are needed. Try to work this one out as we did the Full House: choose the ranks first, then which of those will be the triple, and then the actual cards of each rank.

a) How many different Three of a Kinds are there?

Example: _____

b) What is the probability of being dealt a Three of a Kind?

22.11) **Two Pair** consists of 2 cards of one rank, 2 cards of another rank, and a singleton at a third rank. Again try to work this one as we did the Full House and the Three of a Kind.

a) How many different Two Pairs are there in pinochle poker? **Remember to subtract off the Flushes with Two Pair.**

Example: _____

b) What is the probability of being dealt Two Pairs?

22.12) **One Pair** consists of 2 cards of one rank, and 3 singletons each of a differing rank, so 4 ranks are needed. Try with same method.
a) How many different hands have One Pair in pinochle poker? **Remember to subtract off the Flushes with One Pair.**

Example: _____

b) What is the probability of being dealt One Pair?

22.13) **High Card Only** When you're playing pinochle poker and no one has any of these special poker hands, the hand with the highest card (aces are high) wins and if there's a tie, you move to the 2nd high in those hands, etc. (Look on table.)

a) What is the number of possible high card only hands? Example: _____

b) What is the probability of being dealt no special poker hand and have a High Card Only hand?

22.14) Now we'll rank the five card hands in pinochle poker like we did for regular poker. Here's a list of the hands to consider and put in order: Royal Straight Flush, Straight Flush, 5 of a Kind, 4 of a Kind, Full House, Flush with Two Pairs, Flush with One Pair, Flush with No Pair, Straight, 3 of a Kind, Two Pair, One Pair, and High Card Only.

Pinochle Poker Hand		Number of Each Type of Hand	Probability (4 sig figs)
Tie		128	0.00007475
		128	0.00007475
		336	0.0001962
		480	0.0002803
		512	0.000299
		1920	0.001121
		16,800	0.009811
		47,040	0.02747
		65,280	0.03812
		130,560	0.07625
		215,040	0.1256
		375,840	0.2195
		858,240	0.5021
Total		1,712,304	$1.000897 \approx 1$

22.15) How does this ranking compare to the one for a regular deck of cards? Were there any rankings that surprised you?

22.16) Let's say you decide to play pinochle poker but **ALL OF THE DIAMONDS ARE REMOVED**. Leave your answers as a fraction, no need to reduce.

    a) How many ways are there to choose your 5 cards?

    b) P(Royal Straight Flush)   Example: _____

    c) P(Straight Flush)   Example: _____

    d) P(Five of a Kind)   Example: _____

    e) P(Four of a Kind)   Example: _____

    f) P(Full House)   Example: _____

    g) P(Flush with Two Pair)   Example: _____

h) P(Flush with One Pair)   Example: _____

i) P(Three of a Kind)   Example: _____

22.17) Now let's say you decide to play pinochle poker but **ALL OF THE NINES ARE REMOVED**. Leave your answers as a
fraction, no need to reduce.
    a) How many ways are there to choose your 5 cards?

    b) P(Royal Straight Flush)   Example: _____

    c) P(Four of a Kind)   Example: _____

    d) P(Flush with Two Pair)   Example: _____

    e) P(Flush with One Pair)   Example: _____

    f) P(Straight) (you don't have to subtract off anything)   Example: _____

GROUP #23

Keno and Lotteries

1	2	3	4	5	6	7	8	9	10
11	12	13	14	15	16	17	18	19	20
21	22	23	24	25	26	27	28	29	30
31	32	33	34	35	36	37	38	39	40
41	42	43	44	45	46	47	48	49	50
51	52	53	54	55	56	57	58	59	60
61	62	63	64	65	66	67	68	69	70
71	72	73	74	75	76	77	78	79	80

10 SPOT GAME

Match	Prize
10	$100,000
9	$5000
8	$500
7	$50
6	$10
5	$2
0	$5

Odds: 1 in 9.05

9 SPOT GAME

Match	Prize
9	$25,000
8	$2000
7	$100
6	$20
5	$5
4	$2

Odds: 1 in 6.53

8 SPOT GAME

Match	Prize
8	$10,000
7	$50
6	$10
5	$2
4	$5

Odds: 1 in 9.77

7 SPOT GAME

Match	Prize
7	$2,000
6	$100
5	$11
4	$5
3	$1

Odds: 1 in 4.23

6 SPOT GAME

Match	Prize
6	$1,100
5	$57
4	$7
3	$1

Odds: 1 in 6.19

5 SPOT GAME

Match	Prize
5	$410
4	$18
3	$2

Odds: 1 in 10.34

4 SPOT GAME

Match	Prize
4	$72
3	$5
2	$1

Odds: 1 in 3.86

3 SPOT GAME

Match	Prize
3	$27
2	$2

Odds: 1 in 6.55

2 SPOT GAME

Match	Prize
2	$11

Odds: 1 in 16.63

1 SPOT GAME

Match	Prize
1	$2

Odds: 1 in 4

Keno is a casino version of the lottery. The casino has a container filled with N balls numbered from 1 to N. A player buys a ticket with which they select anywhere a certain amount of those N numbers and marks them with a "spot." Then the casino or lottery commission selects M winning numbers and you see how many you have matched.

For the first 3 problem we will be studying Ohio's OH! lottery version of Keno which is played by buying your ticket at a gas station, etc. In OH! Keno you decide how many spots you want to play (1 to 10). Then the casino (or lottery) mechanically (or computer generated program) **chooses 20 winning numbers** from the 80 possible numbers. If a sufficient number of the player's spots are winning numbers, the player receives an appropriate payoff (noted in the table). We will assume that you pay $1 to play, so you get the given amount of prize money.

23.1) Ohio OH! For this problem **three** spots are marked, the player wins if 2 or 3 of their spots are selected. Put an X through 3 numbers on the above table.

   a) How many total ways can a player select 3 spots from the 80 numbers?

   b)

Outcome	Number of ways	Probability (3 decimal places)
3 matched spots ($27 payout)		
2 matched spots ($2 payout)		
0 or 1 matched ($0 payout)		

   c) The lottery card says that the overall "odds" of winning any money in the 3 spot game are 1 in 6.55. These are not actually odds, they are the probability: 1 in 6.55 means 1/6.55 probability. Verify this is true by adding up the probabilities of the outcomes in which you win money and comparing it to the given "odds.".

23.2) Looking at the "odds" for each game, how many spots gives you the i) best and ii) worst probability of winning something?

23.3) Ohio OH! Now we will play the 1 Spot Game. Choose 1 numbers from 1 to 80. _____
   a)   How many total ways are there to choose your number?

   b)

Outcome	Number of ways	Probability (2 decimal places)
1 matched spot ($2 payout)		
0 matched spots ($0 payout)		

   c) Verify the "odds" of winning are 1 in 4.

23.4) Ohio OH! Now we will play the 2 Spot Game. Choose 2 numbers from 1 to 80. _____ _____
   a) How many total ways are there to choose your numbers?

   b)

Outcome	Number of ways	Probability (2 decimal places)
2 matched spots ($11 payout)		
0 or 1 matched spots ($0 payout)		

   c) Verify the "odds" of winning are 1 in 16.63.

23.5) CREATE YOUR OWN LOTTERY With your group determine the following:

   a) Total numbers to choose from: 1 to _____   b) Amount of winning numbers chosen by the lottery: _____

   c) Amount of losing numbers: _____   d) Amount of numbers patrons will choose (make it more than 4): _____

   e) How many ways are there for a patron to choose their numbers?

   f) P(match all of their numbers)   g) P(none of their numbers)

   h) P(match at least one of their numbers)   i) P(match 2 of their numbers)

114

23.6) POWERBALL Powerball is a lottery game played in 44 States (including IN), D.C., Puerto Rico, and the US Virgin Islands as of 2017. Every Wednesday and Saturday at 10:59 p.m. Eastern Time, 5 white balls were drawn out of a drum with 69 white balls and 1 red ball out of a drum with 26 red balls. Each ticket costs $2. Go to 4 significant figures for probability.

   a) Determine the total number of different Powerball tickets in a given drawing.

   b) P(jackpot) = P(○○○○○ + ●)

   c) P(win $1,000,000) = P(○ ○ ○ ○○)

   d) P(win $100) = P(○ ○○ + ●)

   e) P(getting no money) = P(○ ○ or ○ or no matches)

   f) On www.powerball.com they claimed that the overall "odds" of having a winning ticket is better than 1 in 24.87. Verify that this is true by subtracting the probability of getting no money from 1 and compare.

23.7) A Keno game has you choose 3 numbers from 1 to 50. Then the lottery commission chooses 10 winning numbers and you win money if you match 2 or 3 of the winning numbers.

   a) How many different Keno tickets could you pick?

   b) Fill in the table.

Outcome	Number of ways	Probability (3 decimal places)
3 matched spots ($50 payout)		
2 matched spots ($10 payout)		
0 or 1 matched ($0 payout)		

   c) The back of the Keno card says that the "odds" of winning any money are 1 in 10.2. Verify this.

23.8) In a different keno game, you choose 5 numbers from the numbers 1 through 70 and 15 winning numbers are chosen.
   a) How many different ways are there to choose your 5 numbers?

   b) P(match all 5 of your numbers)   c) P(match 3 of your 5 numbers)

23.9) Back the Ohio OH! This time look at the 4 Spot Game.   Remember there are 80 numbers to chose from and the lottery commission chooses 20 winning numbers.
   a)   How many total ways are there to choose 4 numbers out of 80?

   b)

Outcome	Number of ways	Probability (3 decimal places)
4 matched spots ($72 payout)		
3 matched spots ($5 payout)		
2 matched spots ($1 payout)		
1 or fewer matched ($0 payout)		

   c) Verify the "odds" of winning some money are 1 in 3.86.

23.10) Yet another keno game has you choose 8 numbers from the numbers 1 through 35 and 10 winning numbers are chosen.
   a) How many different ways are there to choose your 8 numbers?

   b) What is the probability that you match all 8?

   c) What is the probability that you match 3 of the 8?

   d) What is the probability that you didn't match any of your numbers?

GROUP #24

Expectation
and
Lotteries

In this group we will see how to determine how much money you can expect to win given a lottery ticket and the prizes offered which is also called the **Expectation** or **Expected Value**. The amount that you find to be the expected value will be the average amount of money you could expect to win if you played it over and over and over again.

EXPECTATION is the sum of each outcome multiplied by its probability

$$EV = E_1 \cdot P(E_1) + E_2 \cdot P(E_2) + \cdots E_n \cdot P(E_n) = \sum_{i=1}^{n} E_i \cdot P(E_i)$$

Since we are dealing with games in this course, expectation (also known as expected value) for us will usually mean how much money we can expect to win or lose playing a game. The easiest way to find the expectation for a game is as follows:

1) **Make a table with first column consisting of all possible outcomes**

2) **Second column consisting of the probability for each outcome**

3) **Third column with the product of the first two (each outcome times its probability).**

4) **To get the expectation, add up the final column and subtract the price to play if there is one.**

A **FAIR GAME** is a game with an expectation of zero. This means if the game is played over and over again, all players are expected to break even (neither lose nor win any money).

Ex1. A game costs $1 to play. You pick a rubber duck from a pond containing 21 of them each with a spot underneath, 1 blue, 3 red, and 17 green. You win $20 if you get the blue, $5 if you get a red, and $0 if you get a green.
   a) Find your expected winnings.

   Outcomes   Probabilities   Product

   b) Would you play this game? Why or why not?

Ex2. You pay $2 to play the following game. You flip a coin 5 times; if all 5 are heads, you get $7; if 4 are heads, you get $2; if 2 or 3 are heads you $1; otherwise you get nothing.
   a) Find your expectation.

   b) Find the price of a ticket to make this a fair game.

117

Now try some expectation problems with your group.

24.1) Looking back at the Keno game from the previous group, determine the expectation for each of the given Spot Games. The price of a ticket is $1.

a) 1 Spot Game

Outcome	Probability	Product
$2 (1 match)	0.25	
$0 (no match)	0.75	

Expectation: _____

b) 2 Spot Game

Outcome	Probability	Product
$11 (2 matches)	0.06	
$0 (0 or 1 match)	0.94	

Expectation: _____

c) What should the price of the ticket be for the 1 Spot Game for it to be fair?

d) What should the price of the ticket be for the 2 Spot Game for it to be fair?

e) Would you play this 1 or 2 Spot Keno game? Why or why not?

24.2) In this keno game, you choose 3 numbers from 1 – 30 and then 10 winning numbers are chosen. You win $15 if you match all 3, $5 if you match 2, and $0 if you match 1 or 0. The price of a ticket is $1.

a) Determine the expected winnings.

Outcome	Probability (leave as fractions)	Product (leave as fractions)
$15 (match 3)		
$5 (match 2)		
$0 (match 1 or 0)		

Expectation _____

b) Would you play this game? Why or why not?

c) What should the price of ticket be so that it will be a fair game?

24.3) HOOSIER LOTTO The Hoosier Lotto is another lottery, but it is only played in the state of Indiana. For this lottery you choose 6 numbers out of 48 numbers and win if you match at least 2 of the chosen 6. Since 2001 instead of drawing balls, the 6 numbers are chosen by a computer using an RNG or Random Number Generator to avoid any human error.

a) Determine the total number of different Hoosier Lotto tickets in a given drawing.

b) Fill in the the table and then determine the expected value of a $1 ticket for the Hoosier Lotto.

	Outcome		Probability leave as fractions	Product ($) · (probability) Round to 3 decimal places
Match	Prize			
6 of 6	Jackpot (say **$1,000,000**)			
5 of 6	approx **$1000** (pari-mutuel)			
4 of 6	approx **$40** (pari-mutuel)			
3 of 6	**$3**			
2 of 6	Free Quick Pick (worth **$1**)			
0 or 1 of 6	**$0**			

Expectation: _____

c) How much money would you expect to win (or lose) if you bought a Hoosier Lotto ticket every day for the next 10 years? Don't worry about leap year.

d) So how much money of the original money you bought the tickets with would you have left after the 10 years?

e) How much $ would you have if you put $1 into a jar in your room every day for the next ten years? Again, don't worry about leap year.

f) Which seems like a better way to use your money?

More expectation problems

24.4) You friend Jim has a game for you to play. You roll a fair die. If you roll a 1, Jim pays you $25. If you roll a 2, Jim pays you $5. If you roll a 3, you win nothing. If you roll a 4 or 5, you must give Jim $10, and if you roll a 6, you must give Jim $15. What is your expected value for this game?

24.5) A game costs $1 to play. After paying the dollar, we roll a pair of dice. If we roll a sum of 7, we get our dollar back (the game is a draw). If we roll a sum of 6 or 8, then we win and are given $3. Otherwise, then we lose our dollar.

a) What is the expected value of this game?

b) In order to make this a fair game, what should the cost be to play?

24.6) A raffle offers a first prize of $1000, 2 second prizes of $300 each, and 20 third prizes of $10 each. There are 10,000 tickets are sold at $0.50 each.

a) What are the expected winnings for a person buying one ticket?

b) What would the expectation be if you bought five tickets?

c) What should the price of the tickets be to make this a fair game?

GROUP #25

Roulette
and
Expected Value

We will go back to Roulette for this group. Recall the roulette wheel has **38** slots consisting of 18 red spaces, 18 black, and 2 green (considered neither even nor odd). Note: If you win, the bet that you've made goes back to you as well the amount from the house odds. If you lose, you lose the money you bet. If you use the True or Actual Odds, Roulette is a fair game so your expectation will be $0.

Ex. If you place a $1 bet on three numbers (a street) and the casino paid you using the house odds (11 to 1), here is how you'd determine the expectation:

<u>Outcome</u>　　　　　　　<u>Probability</u>　　　　　　<u>Product</u>

You can use the table like above or use the following equation which amounts to the same thing:

($ win)(P(win)) – ($ lose)(P(lose)) = expectation for roulette bet

where odds against are given **b to a** or **$ win to $ lose**

Ex. Back to the three number bet, it would look like:

25.1) You place a $1 bet on one number. The house odds are 35 to 1.
　a) What is the probability that you will win this bet?

　b) How much money would you win if your number comes up (not including your bet that remains on the table)?

　c) Determine the expectation for this bet.

25.2) You place a $1 bet on two numbers (a split). The house odds are 17 to 1.
　a) What is the probability that you won't win this bet?

　b) How much money would you win if either of your numbers comes up (not including your bet remaining on the table)?

　c) Determine the expectation for this bet.

25.3) Now you place a $1 bet on two numbers (a split) and the casino decides to use the true odds (18 to 1). (Note: this wouldn't actually happen!) What is the expectation?

25.4) You place a $1 bet on four numbers (a corner) with house odds being 8 to 1.
   a) What are the odds against you winning this bet?

   b) How much money would you lose if your numbers don't come up?

   c) Determine the expectation for this bet.

25.5) For that same $1 bet on four numbers, what if the casino used the actual odds of 8.5 to 1, then what would the expected value?

25.6) You place a $1 bet on five numbers which has house odds of 6 to 1.
   a) What is the probability that you will win this bet?

   b) How much money would you win if your number comes up (not including your bet that remains on the table)?

   c) Determine the expectation for this bet.

25.7) Your friend places a $1 bet on a line (six numbers). The house odds are 5 to 1. What is your friends expectation?

25.8) What is the expectation for a $1 bet on twelve numbers (a column) with house odds given as 2 to 1?

25.9) Finally, if you place a $1 bet on either low/high/even/odd/red/black, you're really betting on eighteen numbers. The house odds are 1 to 1.

   a) What is the probability that you will win this type of bet?

   b) How much money would you win if your number comes up (not including your bet that remains on the table)?

   c) Determine the expectation for this bet.

25.10) Which odds make roulette a fair game? So why do casinos use House odds instead of actual odds?

25.11) Which is the worst bet to make with house odds? How much can you expect to lose for every dollar on this bet? So how much would you expect to lose on a $100 bet?

★★★★★ NOTICE THAT WHEN YOU USE HOUSE ODDS EVERY ROULETTE BET HAS AN EXPECTATION OF LOSING $0.05 OR LOSING $0.08! ★★★★★

Now back to regular expectation problems where you make a table...

25.12) Someone has a weighted coin that lands heads up with probability 2/3 and tails up with probability 1/3. If the coin comes up heads, you pay $1; if the coin comes up tails, you receive $1.50.

   a) What is the expected value for this game?

   b) Would you play? Why or why not?

25.13) Someone has a weighted coin that lands heads up with probability 2/3 and tails up with probability 1/3, but the game has changed. You now pay $5 to flip the coin. If the coin comes up heads, you get nothing. For this game to be a fair game, how much should you receive if you flip tails?

25.14) For several years in Massachusetts, the lottery commission would mail residents coupons for free Lotto tickets. To win the jackpot in MA, you have to correctly guess all six numbers drawn from a pool of 36. What is the expected value of the free Lotto ticket if the jackpot is $8,000,000 and there is no splitting of the prize?

25.15) A friend offers to pay you $25 if you draw the ace of spades and $4 for any other spade. However you must pay your friend $1 for any non-spade drawn. By finding the expected value, determine whether you should accept the offer.

25.16) Now the friend has changed his game and has you grab 2 cards from a deck of cards. If you grab 2 aces he will give you $100. If you grab 2 face cards, he will give you $25. Otherwise you will owe him $2. Find the expected value and determine if you would play this game.

25.17) A school is holding a raffle and sold 900 tickets at $5 each. The winning ticket holder will get $500 and 3 runner-up prizes of $50 each will also be awarded.
    a) What are the expected winnings for a ticket?

    b) What would the tickets cost for this to be a fair raffle?

25.18) A slot machine has 3 reels each with 10 symbols. On each reel there is 1 JACKPOT symbol. You put a dollar in the slot and the payoffs are as follows: 3 JACKPOT symbols pays $487; 2 JACKPOT symbols pays $10; and 1 JACKPOT symbol pays $1 (i.e. you get your wager back). Find the expectation if it costs $1 to play (this will show that this slot machine is fair).

GROUP #26

Blackjack
A Lesson in Counting Cards

Blackjack is essentially a game between two people – the player and the dealer. To win, a player's hand must have a value closer to 21 than the dealer's hand without going over 21. Aces are worth either 1 or 11 (at your discretion), tens, jacks, queens, and kings are each worth 10, and all other cards are worth their face values. (The suits of the cards do not matter.) The term "**blackjack**" means that you get a value of 21 with only two cards (an ace and a card with that is worth 10).

❖ The dealer deals two cards to each player and takes two for themself (first face down and second face up).

❖ A game using one or two decks of cards held in the dealers hand is called a "pitch" game and the players cards are dealt face down.

❖ A game using more decks of cards which are held in a shoe is called a "shoe" game and the players cards are both dealt face up (and they must not touch their cards). This is the way casinos play Blackjack.

❖ Each player in turn may "hit" – take another card – or "stay" / "stand" – not take another card – until they are satisfied with their total or they "bust" with a total exceeding 21. If a player busts, they lose their bet.

❖ After all of the players are done, the dealer then plays out their hand following these rules:
  • The dealer must "hit" if they have 16 or less.
  • The dealer must "stay" (not take a card) if they are 17 or higher.
  • The table might read "Dealer hits on soft 17" which means a hand with an Ace worth 11 and a 6 where you can't bust by taking another card.

❖ If the dealer busts, they pay off all players with hands still alive.

❖ If the dealer reaches 17 or better, they pay off players with higher totals less than or equal to 21. If a player has the same value as the dealer, the game is a PUSH and the player gets his bet back (doesn't lose or win).

❖ The only real advantage for the house is that players have a chance to bust first and if both the player and dealer bust, the house wins.

❖ Often casinos pay 3 to 2 for a "natural" Blackjack in a 6-8 deck game (meaning $10 bet would pay you $15), but now many casinos have started playing single deck blackjack which only pays 6 to 5 for a blackjack (meaning a $10 bet will only pay $12).

For the first two problems, we will assume there is only one deck of cards being used.

26.1) For the dealer, the order of the cards matters because only one card faces up.
  a) How many different pairs of cards can the dealer be dealt (one dealt up and one dealt down)?

  b) Given the dealer is dealt an Ace up, what is the probability that they have a blackjack?

  c) Given the dealer is dealt a card worth 10 up, what is the probability that they have a blackjack?

  d) So why would it matter to if you know the dealer has an Ace or a card worth 10?

125

26.2) For players, order wouldn't matter because they're either both face up or both face down.

   a) How many different pairs of cards can a player be dealt?

   b) How many different Blackjacks are there?

   c) What is the probability of being dealt a blackjack?

26.3) In most casino blackjack games, several decks of cards are used and stored in the shoe.

   a) Do you think the probability of being dealt a blackjack on the first two cards will increase, decrease, or stay the same if more than one deck of cards is used?

   b) Calculate the probability of being dealt a blackjack with the first two cards (an Ace together with a 10/J/Q/K) using the following amount of decks. Remember you need to figure out how many cards there are, how many aces there are and how many cards worth 10 in the number of given decks. (go to 4 significant figures)
      i) **two** decks of cards.

      ii) **three** decks of cards.

      iii) **six** decks of cards (number commonly used at casinos).

PLAY BLACKJACK with your group. Have one member be the dealer for the first round and then rotate who deals. Since you are only using one deck (a pitch game) deal the cards to each player face down but remember that the dealer always gets one face down and one face up.

BASIC STRATEGY

You can increase your odds of winning in blackjack by memorizing the table to the right. It is not illegal or frowned upon; any good blackjack player should know it.

The left column shows what you have in your hand, either by sum (for the first rows) or by the actual combination of cards.

The top row is the one face up card that the dealer has.

You match up what you have and what the dealer is showing to determine what you should do.

H = Hit

D = Double Down (take only one card and double your bet)

S = Stand

P = Split

Your Hand	Dealer's Card									
	2	3	4	5	6	7	8	9	10	A
8 or less	H	H	H	H	H	H	H	H	H	H
9	H	D	D	D	D	H	H	H	H	H
10	D	D	D	D	D	D	D	D	H	H
11	D	D	D	D	D	D	D	D	D	H
12	H	H	S	S	S	H	H	H	H	H
13	S	S	S	S	S	H	H	H	H	H
14	S	S	S	S	S	H	H	H	H	H
15	S	S	S	S	S	H	H	H	H	H
16	S	S	S	S	S	H	H	H	H	H
17	S	S	S	S	S	S	S	S	S	S
A,2	H	H	H	D	D	H	H	H	H	H
A,3	H	H	H	D	D	H	H	H	H	H
A,4	H	H	D	D	D	H	H	H	H	H
A,5	H	H	D	D	D	H	H	H	H	H
A,6	H	D	D	D	D	H	H	H	H	H
A,7	S	D	D	D	D	S	S	H	H	H
A,8	S	S	S	S	S	S	S	S	S	S
2,2	P	P	P	P	P	P	H	H	H	H
3,3	P	P	P	P	P	P	H	H	H	H
4,4	H	H	H	P	P	H	H	H	H	H
5,5	D	D	D	D	D	D	D	D	H	H
6,6	P	P	P	P	P	H	H	H	H	H
7,7	P	P	P	P	P	P	H	H	H	H
8,8	P	P	P	P	P	P	P	P	P	P
9,9	P	P	P	P	P	S	P	P	S	S
10,10	S	S	S	S	S	S	S	S	S	S
A,A	P	P	P	P	P	P	P	P	P	P

COUNTING CARDS

A strategy to improve your odds of winning is the Hi-Lo counting card system which, contrary to common belief, is not illegal. However if a casino notices you doing it, they may have the dealer shuffle the deck more often or even ask you to leave. The strategy is actually quite simple; you just need to pay attention and not get distracted.

You start with your count N = 0 and then add or subtract from it according to:

+ 1 for each card from 2 – 6
0 for each card from 7 – 9
– 1 for each Ace, 10, Jack, Queen, King

N will give you an idea of how many high or low cards are left in the deck- the higher N is the more likely there are high cards left and the more likely the dealer will bust and the lower N is the more likely low cards are left. Most casinos use six decks of cards so you need to figure out about how many high or low cards are left in the shoe, so once you get N, you need to divide it by your estimate of the number of decks left in the shoe.

T = N / approximate # of decks left in the shoe

Then your value for T will help you decide how to bet:

T < 0   →   no bet
0 < T < 1.49   →   minimum bet (base amount)
1.5 < T < 3.49   →   bet 2 times your base amount
3.5 < T < 5.49   →   bet 3 times your base amount
5.5 < T < 7.49   →   bet 4 times your base amount
7.5 < T   →   bet 5 times your base amount

One note is that you need to keep track of your count for hours and once the dealer has shuffled, you have to start over again at 0! This system is quite simple, but the implementation of it requires a lot of work and sometimes a whole team of people.

127

26.4) Try this example: Start with N = 0

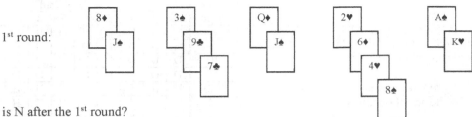

1st round:

a) What is N after the 1st round?

2nd round:

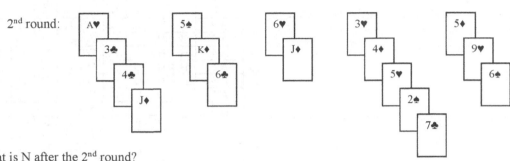

b) What is N after the 2nd round?

c) Say you estimate that there are 5 decks of cards left in the shoe, what is T and how should you bet?

d) If you estimate there are only 2 decks left, what is T and how should you bet?

26.5) You want to play blackjack with some of your friends and have found a shoe that will hold 10 decks of cards.
   a) How many different 2 card hands are possible?

   b) What is the probability that you are dealt a blackjack (an Ace with a 10/J/Q/K)?

Review
26.6) You place a $100 bet on a split (2 numbers) in a game of roulette. Remember the wheel has 38 slots and the house odds for a 2 number bet are 17 to 1.
   a) P(winning your bet)   b) P(losing your bet)   c) What are the odds in favor of winning your bet?

   d) If you win, what is your payout (beyond keeping your bet) from the casino?

   e) If you had only placed a $1 bet on the split (2 numbers), what would your EXPECTED payout be?

REVIEW PROBLEMS FOR TEST 2

1) In a game of Let's Make a Deal, the host offers you a choice of 6 doors, five with a goat behind them and one with a car behind it. The host will then open 4 of the remaining doors which reveal 4 goats and ask you if you want to stay with the door you chose or switch to the other door.

    a) P(car if you stay)   b) P(car if you switch)   c) P(goat if you stay)

    d) P(goat if you switch)   e) Should you stay or switch?

2) Select two cards from a standard deck.

    a) P(both face cards)   b) What are the odds of getting two face cards?

3) What are the odds of drawing a five from a standard deck?

4) One card is drawn from a standard deck. What are the odds it's a club or a jack?

5) The odds are 6:1 against it being sunny today. What's the probability that it will be sunny?

6) Out of 250 students interviewed at a community college, 90 were taking math but not chemistry, 160 were taking math, and 50 were not taking either one. Find the probability that a student chosen at random was:

    a) taking just chemistry   b) taking math or chemistry, but not both

    c) taking chemistry   d) not taking math

    e) taking math, given they were taking chemistry   f) P(taking chemistry | taking math)

    g) P(taking math | chemistry or math)   h) taking chemistry, given they were not taking math

    i) P(not taking math | not taking chemistry)

7) Two letters are chosen at random from NUMERICAL. What's the probability that both are vowels?

8) Two dice are tossed. Determine the following.
   a) P(sum of 9)   b) P(dice show same #)   c) P(dice show different #s)

   d) P(sum of 3 or 7)   e) P(doubles | sum of 8)   f) P(one die is a 3 | sum of 9)

9) In roulette, you bet on 5 numbers and house odds for your payout are 6 to 1. (There are 38 spaces on a roulette wheel.)
   a) What is the probability that you will
        i) win your bet?   ii) lose your bet?

   b) What are the odds
        i) against winning your bet?   ii) in favor of winning your bet?

   c) If you bet $10 and win your bet, how much money will you get (not including your bet will stay on the table)?

   d) What is your expected payout on a $1 bet?

10) A slot machine with 3 reels each with 10 symbols including one jackpot on each reel.
    a) P(3 jackpots)   b) P(1 jackpot)

    c) If there are 3 reels with 10 symbols but now each reel includes 4 jackpots, find P(1 jackpot).

11) A coin is tossed six times. What's the probability of getting:
    a) no heads?   b) exactly one tail?

    c) exactly three heads?   d) at least one head?

12) Four cards are drawn at random from the thirteen hearts in a standard deck. What's the probability the selection contains:
   a) no face cards?

   b) both king and queen?

   c) queen but not king?

   d) at least two face cards?

13) A letter is chosen at random from the alphabet. What's the probability that the letter is in the word "house" or "phone"?

14) Two marbles are drawn at random from a bag containing 3 red, 5 blue, and 6 green marbles. What's the probability of drawing:
   a) no blue?

   b) at least 1 blue?

   c) two of the same color?

   d) two of different colors?

15) A committee of six people is to be selected from a group of seven men and eight women. What's the probability that the committee contains:
   a) at least one woman?

   b) at most one woman?

16) Five cards are drawn at random from a standard deck. Find the probability that:
   a) exactly 2 are hearts.

   b) all are kings or queens.

   c) no face cards.

   d) at least 3 aces.

17) A bag contains five pennies and ten nickels. If three coins are selected at random, what's the probability of getting $0.11?

18) A game costs $1 to play. You flip a coin 5 times in a row and count how many heads you have. If you get 5 heads, then you win $10. If you get 3 or 4 heads, you get $5. If you get anything else, you get nothing!
    a) Find the expected value of this game.

    b) Would you play this game? Why or why not?

19) In a special lottery, 50,000 $1-tickets are sold. The first prize is $15,000 and the five second-prize winners will each get $400. Gerta Gambler buys one ticket.
    a) What is her expectation?

    b) What should the game cost to play in order to be a fair game?

20) In the game of Risk, if the attacker rolls: 5, 4, 3 and the defender rolls: 4, __. List the outcomes as well.
    a) P(attacker losing 2 armies)   b) P(defender losing 2 armies)   c) P(both losing one army)

21) Five cards are drawn from a 48 card pinochle deck. Recall there are 2 of each of the following ranks in each suit: 9, 10, J, Q, K, A. Determine the following.
    a) P(3 jacks)   b) P(both 10 of ♣ but no Aces)

    c) The QUEENS and KINGS are removed from the deck, so there are only 32 cards. Find P(Five of a Kind).

        Example _____

22) Janine and I were playing Scrabble and when she reached in and grabbed her 7 initial letter tiles at the beginning of the game, she got 6 O's! Knowing that of the 100 letter tiles there are only 8 O's, what is the probability that someone would get exactly 6 O's? (Go to 4 significant figures)

23) In a keno game you pay $1 and choose 3 numbers from the numbers 1 - 70. Then the casino chooses 15 winning numbers and you see how many you have matched.
    a) How many total ways can you select 3 numbers from the 70 numbers?

    b) P(match 2 of your numbers)   c) P(match at least 1 of your numbers)

24) Find the probability of getting each type of poker hand when dealt 5 cards from a deck with a FIFTH SUIT added, so there are 65 cards total.
    a) P(Straight Flush)   Example _____

    b) P(One Pair)   Example _____

25) A new medical test can determine whether or not a human has a disease that affects 5% of the population. The test correctly gives a positive result for 99% of the people who have the disease, but gives a false positive for 3% of people who do not have the disease. If a person test positive, what is the probability that the person has the disease?

    a) What are you looking for? P(_____ | _____)

    b) Find the probability.

26) You are playing blackjack with 5 decks of cards and recall a blackjack is an Ace with a 10/J/Q/K.
    a) How many different 2 card hands can you be dealt?   b) P(being dealt a blackjack)

 **COINS and SPOOF**

In this group we will focus on coins. The probability of flipping coins is simple because there are only two possibilities, heads or tails and each time you flip a coin the probability remains the same since the flips are independent of each other. We will start out with some questions about coin probability and then move on to a game.

1) Everyone take a penny and flip it 4 times and count how many heads / tails you get. Do this 10 times and record how many times you get each of the following outcomes.

Outcomes	Occurrence tallies	# of occurrences at your table	Total occurrencs in class	Probabilites
0H / 4T				
1H / 3T				
2H / 2T				
3H / 1T				
4H / 0T				
		Total flips		

2) Now we'll look at the theoretical probabilities when you flip a coin 4 times in a row.
   a) How many different outcomes are there?

   b) List the outcomes where you get:
      i) no heads which is the same as 4C0.   ii) get 1 head which is the same as 4C1.

      iii) 2 heads which is the same as 4C2.   iv) 3 heads which is the same as 4C3.

      v) 4 heads which is the same as 4C4.

   c) Find the probabilities of the following when flipping a coin 4 times (and write as decimals to compare to our results).
      i) P(0H)   ii) P(1H)   iii) P(2H)

      iv) P(3H)   v) P(4H)

   d) Compare these probabilities to the trials we did. Are they similar?

The game Spoof is typically a pub game where the loser will buy a round of drinks. No one knows the exact origin, but the present day game has its origins in the Cotswolds in England in the late 60s and early 70s.

THE RULES OF SPOOF:

- Every player has 3 coins which they hold in their lap.

- At the beginning of a round each player places 0, 1, 2, or 3 of their coins in their fist and holds it in the middle of the table.

- In turn everyone guesses how many total coins are represented in the hands in the middle (for a 4 player game there could be anywhere from 0 coins to 12) without repeating any previous guess.

- Everyone reveals how many coins they are holding and if someone guessed the correct sum, they are out of the round or safe. If no one guesses the correct amount, then everyone stays in.

- Rounds keep going until there is only one person left who has lost.

Play a game of Spoof until there is only one person left.

3) Were there any good strategies you found for winning?

4) What is the average total of coins in each person's hand?

5) Say you are down to 2 people playing Spoof each with 3 coins.
   a) What are the possible totals? How many different outcomes are there to get those totals?

   b) List the possible outcomes for how many coins each person could have in their hand (have person 1's number of coins first and then person 2's second; for example 0/0).

   c) Determine the probability of each coin total happening.
      i) P(0)   ii) P(1)   iii) P(2)   iv) P(3)

      v) P(4)   vi) P(5)   vii) P(6)

   d) Without considering how many coins you have in your hand, what is your best guess for the total?

e) Knowing that you decide to have 2 coins in your hand, what are the following probabilities?

      i) P(0 given you have 2)   ii) P(1 given you have 2)   iii) P(2 given you have 2)

      iv) P(3 given you have 2)   v) P(4 given you have 2)   vi) P(5 given you have 2)

      vii) P(6 given you have 2)   viii) So is there a best guess?

6) Now say there are 3 people playing Spoof each with 3 coins.

    a) What are the possible totals? How many different outcomes are there?

    b) List the possible outcomes for how many coins each person could have in their hand for the following totals. (Notice that the number of outcomes for these five totals will be half of the all of the outcomes, so the other totals will be similar.)

      i) 0   ii) 1   iii) 2

      iv) 3   v) 4

    c) Determine the probability of each coin total happening.

      i) P(0)   ii) P(1)   iii) P(2)   iv) P(3)

      v) P(4)   vi) P(5)   vii) P(6)   viii) P(7)

      ix) P(8)   x) P(9)

d) Without considering how many coins you have in your hand, what is the best guess for the total?

e) If you are the first person to make your guess, what would be your best guess if you have in your hand:
   i) 0 coins?   ii) 1 coin?   iii) 2 coins?   iv) 3 coins?

f) If you are the second person to make your guess and the first person has guessed 3, what do you think would be your best guess if you have 2 coins in your hand:

Now we'll go back to some problems about just flipping coins...

7) You flip a penny 11 times in a row.
   a) How many different outcomes are there?   b) P(3 tails)   c) P(0 heads)

   d) P(at least 9 tails)   e) P(at least 1 H)

8) Your friend hands you a Susan B. Anthony silver dollar and tells you to flip it 50 times. (Go to 4 significant figures)
   a) What is the probability that you get 25 heads and 25 tails?

   b) What is the probability that you get somewhere between 23 and 27 heads (including 23 and 27)?

   c) What is the probability that you get at least 1 head?

FINAL REVIEW TOPICS

I. **LOGIC** (Groups 1-6)

    A. Puzzles

    B. Sudoku (6)

II. **SETS** (Groups 7-9)

    A. Definitions (union, intersection, number of subsets, etc)

    B. Venn Diagrams

III. **COMBINATORICS** (Groups 10-14)

    A. Order matters- Permutations

    B. Order doesn't matter- Combinations

    C. Coins

    D. Deck of Cards, etc. (7 and 13)

    E. Tournaments (14)

IV. **PROBABILITY** (Groups 15-26)

    A. Odds (notes)

    B. Complement: P(at least one) = 1 – P(none) (notes)

    C. Monty Hall (15)

    D. Slot Machines (16)

    E. Pair of Dice (17)

    F. Risk (17)

    G. Conditional probability (notes)

    H. Roulette (18 and 25)

    I. Bayes Theorem (19)

    J. Poker (20-21)

    K. Pinochle Poker (22)

    L. Lotteries (23-24)

    M. Expectation / Expected Value (24-25)

    N. Blackjack (26)

Be sure to go over your old quizzes and tests and look through the whole workbook; everything is fair game!

FINAL REVIEW PROBLEMS

1) At the local butcher's shop, there were five customers in the lineup. Each of the customers bought something different. The first names of the customers were Annie, Jessica, Lily, Maggie and Naomi. Their last names were Bore, Hazlitt, Piggott, Sowter and Trotter. The available products were: Cumberland sausage, pork chops, pork pie, scotch eggs, and sliced ham.

Lily Piggott was served later than the customer who requested the sliced ham, but before Mrs. Sowter.
The second customer was Maggie.
The pork pie was purchased by the customer directly after Jessica.
Naomi was the woman who bought the scotch eggs; she was served sometime after Annie.
The Cumberland sausage was requested by Mrs. Trotter.
Mrs. Hazlitt was the third in line.
The fourth customer in the line bought the pork chops

Order	1st	2nd	3rd	4th	5th
First name					
Last name					
Product					

2) In a game of Bulls and Cows, the following guesses have been made with the responses. Determine the 3-digit code given that BULL = correct digit in the right position and COW = correct digit in the wrong position.

Guess	# of Bulls	# of Cows
1 2 3	1	0
4 5 6	0	1
7 8 9	0	1
1 4 8	1	0
1 7 4	0	1
7 2 6	0	0

CODE: _____ _____ _____

3) Fill in the Sudoku.

	4		2		
6	2				
	5			3	
	1			6	
1				5	4
			3		

4) Suppose $n(A) = 32$, $n(B) = 91$, and $n(A \cup B) = 100$, find $n(A \cap B)$.

139

5) Given: $U = \{e, f, g, h, i, j, k, l, m, n, o, p\}$, $A = \{f, h, i\}$, $B = \{k, l, p\}$, and $C = \{i, k, l, m, n, o, p\}$.

   a) TRUE or FALSE $i \in C$

   b) TRUE or FALSE $A \subseteq B$

   c) TRUE or FALSE $\emptyset \subseteq A$

   d) $\emptyset^c =$ _____

   e) $A \cup C =$ _____

   f) $A \cap B =$ _____

   g) $n(C) =$ _____

   h) $C^c =$ _____

   i) Find $B \cup (A \cup C)^c$

   j) List the subsets of B.

   k) How many subsets does set C have?

6) Use set notation to describe the shaded area in the Venn diagram.

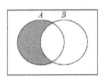

7) If $U = \{ 1, 2, 3, 4, 5, 6, 7, 8, 9 \}$; $R = \{ 2, 4, 6, 8 \}$ and $S = \{ 3, 5, 7 \}$, then determine $R^C \cap S^C$.

8) Shade the region on the Venn Diagram and state in words what they represent if A = those who eat apples, B = those who eat bananas, and C = those who eat cantaloupe.

   a) $(A \cup C)^c$

   i)

   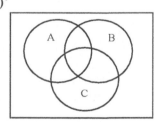

   ii) describe

   b) $B^c \cap C$

   i)

   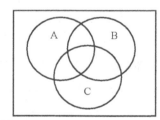

   ii) describe

9) Dr. Holmes surveyed the 38 students in her class about their families. 28 students have a brother or a sister, 15 students have a brother, and 8 students have both a brother and a sister. How many students have a sister?

10) The morning line odds *against* High Limit to win the Kentucky Derby are 10 to 1. What is the *probability* that High Limit *will win* the Derby?

11) An activities director for a cruise ship has surveyed passengers. Of the 280 passengers, fill in each area of the Venn diagram with the appropriate number of people letting S = swimming, D = dancing and G = games.

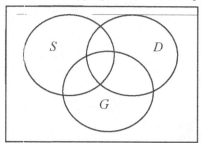

135 like swimming
80 like games
50 liked dancing but *not swimming*
70 like swimming and dancing *but not games*
45 like swimming and games
25 like dancing and games
10 like all three

a) How many liked either swimming or games?

b) How many liked swimming and dancing?

c) How many liked 2 of the 3 types of activities?

d) How many liked games and dancing but not swimming?

12) How many different license plates are possible if they consist of 3 letters followed by 2 digits if repetition is not allowed?

13) From a group of 6 men and 3 women, how many committees of 2 men and 2 women can be formed?

14) A photographer wishes to display four snapshots in a row picked from nine which they have decided are their best. How many ways can this be done?

15) In how many ways can six people be selected from a group of twelve people?

16) Four married couples attend a concert. How many ways can the couples be seated in a row if each couple must be seated together?

17) Given the probability of winning a soccer game is 8/13, what are the odds that you'll lose the game?

18) If you flip a coin 8 times, what is the probability of getting at least 6 heads?

19) A single card is drawn from a deck. What's the probability of selecting
   a) a spade and 3?   b) a 7 or face?   c) a Jack or red?

   d) a 10 given it's not a face?   e) queen given it's not a club?

20) What are the possible outcomes in a best of 3 series between teams A and team B?

21) In the game of Risk, if the attacker rolls: 4, 4, 2 and the defender rolls: 3, ___. List the outcomes as well.
a) P(attacker losing 2 armies)   b) P(defender losing 2 armies)   c) P(both losing one army)

22) Five cards are drawn from a standard deck.
   a) P(exactly one queen)   b) P(at least one diamond)

   c) P(Two Pair)   Example _____

23) A deck of pinochle cards consists of 48 cards with 12 cards of each suit, consisting of two 9's, two 10's, two J's, two Q's, two K's, and two A's. Five cards are drawn from a pinochle deck. (You do not have to subtract any hands.)
   a) P(exactly one queen)   b) P(at least one diamond)

   c) P(Two Pair)   Example _____

24) 100 students are surveyed; 50 say they like math, 30 say they like English, and 20 say they like both. What's the probability a student likes English given they don't like math?

25) A pair of dice is tossed.
    a) P(sum is less than 5)   b) P(one die is 3 | sum is less than 5)

26) If four marbles are drawn from 5 blue, 3 red, and 6 white, what is the probability that at least 3 are blue?

27) There are 38 slots on a roulette wheel. You place a $1 bet on a corner (4 numbers).
    a) What is the probability you will win your bet?   b) What are odds against you winning your bet?

    c) The house odds are 8 to 1. What are your expected winnings using the house odds?

    d) You bet $10 on a corner. Using the house odds, how much money would you net if you win your bet?

28) In a game, a coin is flipped twice. If they get any heads, the player wins $4; if they flip tails twice, the player loses $2.
    a) What is the expected value of this game?

    b) Would you play this game? Why or why not?

29) A hat contains 28 names, 11 of which are male. If three names are randomly drawn from the hat, what is the probability that at least one male name is drawn?

30) A bag consists of the following: 5 red marbles, 3 yellow marbles, and 7 green marbles.
   a) What is the probability that when you reach in and grab 3 balls that you get 2 red and 1 yellow?

   b) What is the probability that when you grab 3 marbles one at a time without replacement that you choose a red, yellow and then another red?

31) A pharmaceutical company has developed a test for a condition that is present in 20% of the population. The test is 90% accurate in determining a positive result for those who have the condition and the chance that a person who doesn't have the condition is given a positive result 5% of the time (known as a false positive). What is the probability that someone who tests positive actually has the condition?

   a) Find P(|)

   b) Determine the probability.

32) You are playing a card game with a standard 52 card deck. You pay $2.00 to play the game. If you choose a red face card you will win $6.00, if you choose a black face card you will win $4.00, if you choose any other card, you will win nothing.
   a) Calculate your expected winnings.

   b) What should the price be to play this game to make it a fair game?

33) A lotto game lets you pick 5 numbers from the numbers 1 through 30 and then 10 winning numbers are chosen.
   a) How many different lottery tickets can you choose?

   b) P(match all 5)   c) P(match 3 of the 5)

34) What is the probability of being dealt a blackjack with 7 decks of cards? Recall that a blackjack consists of an Ace together with a 10, Jack, Queen, or King.

35) A slot machine has 5 reels each with 10 symbols one of which is a jackpot.
   a) How many outcomes are possible?

   b) P(no jackpots)   c) P(3 jackpots)

   d) What is the probability that you will at least one jackpot?

36) Monty Hall offers you a choice of 12 doors, one has a car behind it and eleven have goats behind them. After you choose, Monty will open 10 remaining doors with a goat behind them and then offer you to stay with your original door or swtich. What would you do and why? Use probability.

ANSWERS

TEST 1

Group 2 2.5)a)174 b)645 c)629 d)401 e)052 f)861 g)293 h)358

Group 3 3.1)a)iv b)v c)iv d)iv e)ii f)2 g)Carmine and Frank   3.2)a)D b)B c)A d)C e)D   3.3)a)5 b)D c)ii d)v   3.4)a)2 b)ii c)1 d)3;5   3.5)a)iv b)J, N c)P, M, L d)ii e)v   3.6)a)B b)D c)C d)D e)A   3.7)a)C b)D

Group 4   4.1)

Anne	Carlos	Clive	Margaret	Stephen
Evans	Brown	Harrison	Kelly	Atkins
Matches	Nets	Servers	Worthies	Racquets
18	43	55	30	61

4.2)

1st	2nd	3rd	4th
EMD	AP	OFTM	GG
7	5	2	6
Pink	G&B	P&W	B&W

4.3)Mrs. Peacock with the rope in the library

4.4)

Bob	Master Key	Bedroom	60
Betty	Now and Then	$0	20
Sue	Cliff Hangers	trip	40
Tom	Dice Game	car	50
Lindsay	Plink	$10,000	30

4.5)

order	1st	2nd	3rd	4th	5th	6th	7th	8th	9th	10th
prize	$2500	$5000	$500	$20	$10,000	$100	$10	$1000	$1	$0.01
case #	9	4	7	2	3	1	10	6	8	5

4.6)

level	1	2	3	4	5	6	7	8	9
challenge	movin on up	bobblehead	sticky	balance	egg tower	keep it up	bottoms up	backflip	uphill battle
time	32	27	46	39	43	41	58	52	60
object	cups	pedometer	bread	salt	paper towel	feathers	yo-yo	pencils	marbles

Group 5 HW: 5.1)

Name	Piece	Place
Aaden	Iron	Baltic
Rachel	Thimble	Kentucky
Karen	Ship	Pennsylvania
Colin	Cannon	Boardwalk
Laura	Dog	Marvin Gardens
Scott	Racecar	Jail
Joel	Wheelbarrow	State
Billy	Moneybag	B & O RR

5.2)

1892	1915	1930	1959	1978	1994	1996	2007
James	Jess	Max	George	Muhammad	Mike	Sultan	Ingemar
Corbett	Willard	Schmeling	Foreman	Ali	Tyson	Ibragimov	Johansson
25	35	70	81	61	58	24	28
16	26	56	76	56	50	22	26

Group 6: 6.1)

1	2	4	3
3	4	2	1
2	1	3	4
4	3	1	2

6.2)a)

1	2	4	3
3	4	2	1
4	3	1	2
2	1	3	4

b)

3	2	1	4
4	1	2	3
1	4	3	2
2	3	4	1

c)

1	3	2	4
2	4	1	3
4	1	3	2
3	2	4	1

d)

2	4	1	3
3	1	4	2
1	2	3	4
4	3	2	1

6.3)a)

1	2	3	4	5	6
4	5	6	2	3	1
6	4	2	3	1	5
3	1	5	6	4	2
2	3	1	5	6	4
5	6	4	1	2	3

b)

1	3	6	2	4	5
4	2	5	3	1	6
3	5	1	6	2	4
6	4	2	5	3	1
5	1	3	4	6	2
2	6	4	1	5	3

6.4)

2	9	3	7	1	5	6	8	4
6	4	7	3	8	9	1	5	2
1	8	5	2	4	6	7	9	3
9	7	8	1	5	2	3	4	6
5	3	2	4	6	7	9	1	8
4	1	6	8	9	3	2	7	5
8	2	4	9	3	1	5	6	7
3	5	9	6	7	4	8	2	1
7	6	1	5	2	8	4	3	9

6.5)

5	7	3	8	1	9	6	2	4
8	1	6	4	2	7	3	9	5
9	4	2	6	5	3	7	8	1
6	2	8	3	4	1	5	7	9
7	5	4	9	6	2	1	3	8
1	3	9	5	7	8	2	4	6
2	6	7	1	8	4	9	5	3
3	8	5	2	9	6	4	1	7
4	9	1	7	3	5	8	6	2

3	5	8	9	7	6	4	1	2
1	4	7	2	5	3	6	8	9
6	9	2	1	8	4	7	5	3
4	7	9	5	3	1	2	6	8
2	6	1	8	9	7	3	4	5
8	3	5	6	4	2	1	9	7
5	2	6	7	1	8	9	3	4
9	1	3	4	2	5	8	7	6
7	8	4	3	6	9	5	2	1

SETS AND VENN DIAGRAMS: 1)a){1,2,3,4,5,7} b)∅ c){1,6,7,8,9} d)5 e){6,8,9} f)F g)T h)F   2)a){Kim} b){A,B,E,J,K,S} c){B,D,E,J} d){A,D,S} e){A,B,E,J,K,S} f){K} g){A,S} h){B,E,J,K,D} i){D}   3)a){red} b){blue,green,orange,yellow,purple,white} c){red,orange,blue} d){red,blue,green,orange,white} e)orange,white} f){yellow,purple}   4)a)3 b)20 c)13 d)10 e)10 f)15 g)22 h)5   5)a)440 b)700   6)10   7)a)40 b)16 c)19 d)35 e)81   8)a)60 b)23 c)40 d)72   9)a)19 b)49 c)57 d)61 e)76   10)a)100 b)30 c)20   11)a)450 b)390 c)485 d)370

Group 7: 7.1)a)52 b)red: hearts ♥ and diamonds ♦; black: spades ♠ and clubs ♣ c)26 d)13 e)Ace, 2, 3, 4, 5, 6, 7, 8, 9, 10, Jack, Queen, King f)4 g)Jack, Queen, King h)12   7.2)a)16 b)16 c)32 d)1 e)8 f)3 g)4 h)6 i)12 j)0 k)26 l)12 m)6 n)26   7.3)e)2, 4, 8, 16 f)2^N 7.4)a)32 b)256, so yes c)10 d)64 7.5)a)two sections of P that are not in S; $P \cap S^C$ b)two sections between S and B; $S \cap B$ c)nothing in the P circle or the B circle, but everything else; $(P \cup B)^C$ d)i)those who do not like both solitaire and poker; $(S \cap P)^C$ ii)those who like solitaire or bridge; $S \cup B$ iii)those who like bridge but not solitaire or poker; $B \cap (S \cup P)^C$ 7.6)a)5∪face,16   b)♥∩face,3 c)(red∪♣)^C,13   d)red∩J^C,24 e)(face∩black)∩Q^C,4 f)(3∪♠)∩♥^{C},15   7.7)a)everything in the S circle as well as everything in the P circle; P∪S b)everything but the P circle; P^C c)two sections of B that are not in P; B∩P^C d)like poker and bridge, P∩B e)like none of the three games,(S∪B∪P)^C f)don't like all 3 games,(P∩B∩S)^C

147

Group 8:   8.1)1   8.2)9   8.3)8   8.4)225   8.5)a)72(0 in intersection)   b)47(25 in intersection)   c)25(same Venn as b) d)0(same Venn as a)   8.6)5   8.7)3   8.8) 8.9)a)342 b)192 c)72 d)86   8.10)a)35(0 in all intersections) b)16(7 in middle and 0 outside of C)   c)7(similar to Venn in b)   d)0(similar to Venn in a)   8.11)a)275 b)78 c)16   8.12)a)27 b)66   c)16   8.13)a)70(70 in intersection) b)0(0 in intersection)   c)168(same Venn as b) d)98(same Venn as a)   8.14)a)14 b)4 c)6 d)12 e)8 f)11 g)5 h)15

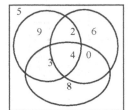

Group 9: 9.1)i)play L, S, and B   ii)play L and S but not B   iii)play L and B but not S   iv)play S and B but not L   v)play only L   vi)play only S   vii)play only B   viii)plays none of the 3   i+ii)plays L and S   ii+v)plays L but not B   iii+v+vii)plays L or B but not S   9.2)i)L∩S∩B   ii)L∩S∩B^C iii) L∩B∩S^C iv) S∩B∩L^C v)L∩(SUB)^C=L∩S^C∩B^C vi)S∩(LUB)^C=S∩L^C∩B^C vii)B∩(LUS)^C=B∩L^C∩S^C viii)(LUSUB)^C=L^C∩S^C∩B^C i+ii)L∩S   ii+v)L∩B^C iii+v+vii)LUB∩S^C 9.5){2,4,*b*,*d*}   9.6){*d*,*f*,*h*}   9.7)b){*a*,*c*,*e*,*g*,*i*,*j*}   c){*b*,*c*,*e*,*g*}   d){*f*,*g*,*h*,*i*}   9.8)b){*c*,*d*,*e*,*h*}   c){*b*,*e*,*f*,*h*} d){*c*,*f*,*g*,*h*}   9.9)a)481   b)704   9.10)a){f,g,h,i,j}   b){c,d,e}   c){a,b,c,d,e,f,g,h}   d)6   e)32   f){b,i,j}   g)∅,{a},{f},{a,f} h){a,f,i,j}   i)*U*   j)T   9.11)a)16   b)6   c)26   9.12)a)i)like bananas but not apples   ii)B ∩ A^C b)i)the 3 sections in A or C that are not in B   ii)(A U C) ∩ B^C 9.13)a)128   b)1024

INTRO TO COMBINATORICS: 1)a)216   b)120   c)40   d)144   2)160   3)12   4)12   5)256   6)720 7)100,000   8)2646   9)512 10)96   11)90   12)5832   13)120   14)12   15)24   16)1,048,576   17)32   18)52 19)11,232,000   20)36   21)a)1 b)4 c)6 d)4 e)1   22)16   23)a)100,000 b)4

Group 11:   11.1)a)3 b)6 c)6 d)3 e)1 f)2   11.2)a)4 b)12 c)24 d)24 e)6 f)4 g)1 h)6   11.3)a)5 b)1 c)3 d)6 e)10 f)3 g)6 h)10 i)5 j)1   11.4)a)3 b)6 c)12   11.5)a)720 b)1000 c)360 d)500 11.6)a)5040 b)10,000 c)5000 d)1680 11.7)a)30,240 b)100,000 c)336 d)6720   11.8)90,720

PERMUTATIONS AND COMBINATIONS: 1)1.5820x10^{10} 2)a)3,628,800 b)362,880   3) 924   4)a)924 b)180   c)378   d)112   5) a)11,400   b)3003   6)a)455 b)91   c)286   d)66   7)507,739,375   8)a)20 b)720 c)840 d)34,650   9)792   10)575,757   11)a)210   b)35   12)2401   13)a)120   b)12   c)24   d)12   14)a)376,992 b)22,957,480   c)5/36 since more chance of winning   15)34   16)a)1365   b)32,760   17)91   18)2,522,520 19)a)7,880,400 b)1,313,400   20)360   21)a)362,880 b)288 c)1728 d)i)15,120 ii)144   22)a)1,000,000,000 b)81 c)43,008   23)560

Group 12:   12.1)20   12.2)120   12.3)336   12.4)35   12.5)120   12.6)15   12.7)40,320   12.8)259,459,200   12.9)165 12.10)2,598,960   12.11)324   12.12)8   12.13)4   12.14)2652   12.15)720   12.16)6   12.17)1000   12.18)286   12.19)60 12.20)40   12.21)970,200   12.22)2.788x10^{10} 12.23)120   12.24)8008   12.25)42   12.26)105   12.27)24   12.28)64,350 12.29)7776 12.30)60   12.31)630   12.32)a)220 b)84 c)6 d)720 e)140 f)40   12.33)a)79,833,600 b)100,800 c)604,800 d)161,280

Group 13: 13.1)2,598,960   13.2)65,780   13.3)65,780   13.4)1287   13.5)845,000   13.6)575,757   13.7)202,800   13.8)22,308   13.9)9295   13.10)712,842   13.11)27,885   13.12)454,480   13.13)1,645,020   13.14)29,172   13.15)24   13.16)4   13.17)48   13.18)2,490,624   13.19)4512   13.20)792   13.21)1,712,304   13.22)886,656   13.23)652,080   13.24)249,900   13.25)2,349,060   13.26)73,815   13.27)79,464   13.28)40   13.29)624   13.30)5148   13.31)1024   13.32)a)4   b)6   c)4   d)1   e)16   f)2^4 13.33)a)32   b)i)1   ii)5   iii)10   iv)1   13.34)a)2^n b)nCr

Group 14: 14.1)a)3 b)7 c)11   d)99   e)N-1   14.2)a)2 or 3   b)4 or 5   c)20 or 21   d)180 or 181   e)2(N-1) or 2(N-1)+1   f)winning team goes undefeated or loses one game   14.3)a)3, 4, or 5   b)15, 16, or 17   c)30, 31, or32   d)270, 271, or 272   e) 3(N-1), 3(N-1)+1, or 3(N-1)+2   14.4) SS, SDS, SDD, DD, DSS, DSD   14.5) SSS, SSDS, SSDDS, SSDDD, SDSS, SDSDS, SDSDD, SDDSS, SDDSD, SDDD, DDD, DDSD, DDSSD, DDSSS, DSDD, DSDSD, DSDSS, DSSDD, DSSDS, DSSS   14.6)a)3 b)6 c)10 d)NC2   14.8)67   14.9)134 or 135   14.10)a)16, 17, 18, or 19 b)40, 41, 42, or 43 c)4(N-1), 4(N-1)+1, 4(N-1)+2, or 4(N-1)+3

TEST 1 REVIEW: 1)

	1st	2nd	3rd	4th
	Ben	James	Nigel	Vicky
	Jones	Best	Stevens	Andrews
	fruit	chocolate	sponge	cheese

2)$A \cap B^C$ 3)a)T b)Ø,{7} c)T d){3,5} e)16 f) Ø   g){1,3,4,5,6,7} h)T i)⊆ j)F k)F l)F m){3,5} n)6   4)190   5)a)1130 b)1910 c)500 d)280   6)all except 2 sections of B that are not in A   7)

2	3	6	5	4	1
4	5	1	2	3	6
1	2	3	4	6	5
5	6	4	3	1	2
3	1	5	6	2	4
6	4	2	1	5	3

8)a)4 b)6 c)Z and Y   9)a)990 b)165   10)a)1287 b)264 c)21,420 d)454,480   11)a)924 b)180 c)378 d)112   12)144   13)a)216 b)120 c)80 d)72   14)503   15)a)13 b)26 or 27   16)a)0 b)16   c)15   17)a)479,001,600 b)604,800 c)103,680   18)a)128 b)35   19)15   20)a)those who like bananas or cantaloupe but not apples b)B ∪ C ∩ A^C

TEST 2

PROBABILITY PROBLEMS: 1)a)46,656 b)0.0000214   2)10/32   3)a)715/8192 b)1093/8192   4)11/26   5)3/11   6)a)Y:2/3, RS:5/7 b)Red Sox   7)a)4to48 b)40to12 c)28to24 d)50to2   8)a)2/30 b)2to28   9)a)12/50 b)3/50   10)a)1/45 b)28/45 c)17/45   11)3/21   12)4/22,100   13)18/27   14)671/1296   15)a)6/120 b)10/120 c)21/120 d)66/120 e)54/120 f)83/120   16)32/51   17)a)1/1947792 b)1/3,838,380   18)a)21/128 b)21/128 c)29/128 d)127/128   19)a)5005/177,100   b)18,564/177,100   c)22,050/177,100   d)28,560/177,100   e)35,035/177,100   f)158,536/177,100   20)a)72/1326 b)376/1326 c)330/1326 d)12/1326   21)a)0.3487 b)0.001488 c)8.258×10^{-4} d)1.613×10^{-5} e)9.072×10^{-6}

Group 15: 15.4)1/3   15.5)2/3   15.6)switch   15.8)a)1/3 b)1/3 c)2/3 d)2/3   15.11)a)1/4 b)3/4 c)3/4 d)1/4 e)switch   15.12)a)4/5 b)4/5 c)1/5 d)1/5   15.13)a)1/10 b)1/10 c)9/10 d)9/10   15.14)a)1/N b)(N−1)/N c)1/N d)(N-1)/N e)switch   15.15)a)4:1 b)1:7 c)28:72   15.65)a)14:3 b)29:11 c)2:8   15.17)a)5/16 b)3/5 c) 9/14   15.18)a)5/9 b))1/10 c)9/11   15.19)48:4   15.20)84:16   15.10)2/11   15.22)3:5   15.23)4:32

Group 16: 16.1)a)4096 b)1/4096 c)2401/4096 d)1372/4096 e)294/4096   16.2)a)65,536 b)1/65,536 c)6561/65,536

16.3)a)1000   b)i)1/1000   ii)27/1000   iii)28/1000   iv)729/1000   16.4)a)14,641   b)10,000/14,641   c)40/14,641

d)4641/14,641 e)41/14,641   16.5)a)16.807 b)7776/16,807 c)6480/16,807 d)2160/16,807 e)360/16,807 f)30/16,807

g)1/16,807   16.6)a)50,625   b)81/50,625   c)20,736/50,625   d)20,736/50,625   e)7776/50,625   f)1296/50,625

g)29,889/50,625   16.7)a)8000   b)24/8000   c)4896/8000   d)3104/8000   e)448/8000   f)2632/8000   g)7528/8000

16.8)a)1000 b)216/1000 c)343/1000 d)657/1000 e)108/1000   16.9)a)279,936 b)78,125/279,936 c)109,375/279,936

d)21,875/279,936 e)4375/279,936

Group 17: 17.1)36   17.2)a)6/36 b)1/36 c)2/36 d)3/36 e)4/36 f)5/36 g)6/36 h)5/36 i)4/36 j)3/36 k)2/36 l)1/36

m)5/36 n)10/36 o)10/36   17.3)a)6;1/6 b)1,2;2/6 c)3,4,5;3/6   17.4)a)0 b)3,4,5,6;4/6 c)1,2;2/6   17.5)a)1;1/6

b)4,5,6;3/6 c)2,3;2/6   17.6)a)8/36 b)4/36 c)24/36 d)6/36 e)30/36 f)6/36, no   17.7)a)30/36 b)18/36 c)11/36

d)25/36 e)21/36 f)15/36 g)1/36 h)10/36 i)25/36   17.8)7; it has the highest probability of all of the sums   17.9)a)0

b)1,2,3,4,5;5/6 c)6;1/6   17.10)a)1,2;2/6 b)5,6;2/6 c)3,4;2/6   17.11) a)3,4,5,6;4/6 b)0/6 c)1,2;2/6   17.12)a)216

b)6/216 c)1/216 d)125/216 e)91/216 f)15/216 g)75/216   17.13)a)400 b)2-40 c)20/400 d)1/400 e)7/400

CONDITIONAL PROBABILITY PROBLEMS: 1)a)1/8 b)4/8 c)6/8 d)3/8 e)7/8 f)1/64 g)1/4 h)2/5 i)0 j)3/5

2)a1/5 b)2/6 c)1/6 d)2/10   3)a)6/54 b)14/44 c)14/20 d)6/20 e)0 f)78/80 g)78/98   4)a)40/250 b)160/250

c)90/250 d)50/120 e)70/110 f)40/130   5)a)4/12 b)0 c)12/48 d)4/40 e)2/20   6)a)1050/2300 b)2100/13800   7)a)9/40

b)4/30 c)24/75   8)a)4/15 b)6/11   9)a)286/2600 b)20/2600 c)4/9880 d)2314/9139   10)1/26

Group 18: 18.3)a)$370;$350 b)$180;$170 c)$116.70;$110 d)$85;$80 e)$66;$60 f)$53.30;$50 g)$21.70;$20

h)$11.10;$10   18.4)a)1/18 b)2/18 c)6/12 d)9/18 e)7/12 f)1/18 g)5/18 h)0 i)1 j)1 k)6/18 l)5/9 m)4/7 n)0

18.5)a)3/38 b)35 to 3 c)$220   18.6)a)26/38 b)12 to 26 c)$100   18.7)a)160,000 b)104,976/160,000 c)16/160,000

d)576/160,000 e)55,024/160,000   18.8)a)32/66 b)32/192

Group 19:   19.1)P(DU|−);0.9863   19.2)P(H|+);0.8103   19.3)P(B|JP);0.1695   19.4)a)P(NY|D);0.4615

b)P(NY|ND)0.2888   19.5)a)P(S|F);0.279 b)P(NS|NF);0.1507   19.6)P(B|F);0.3243   19.7)a)0.6208 b)0.0833 c)0.2959

19.8)a)3/36 b)2/3   19.9)a)1/7 b)6/7 c)6/7 d)1/7 e)switch   19.10)a)6/38 b)32 to 6 c)$125

Group 20:   20.4)1287/2,598,960   20.5)65,780/2,598,960   20.6)22,308/2,598,960   20.7)24/2,598,960

20.8)4512/2,598,960   20.9)575,757/2,598,960   20.10)454,480/2,598,960   20.11)2,357,862/2,598,960

20.12)658,008/2,598,960   20.13)1,940,952/2,598,960   20.14)249,900/2,598,960   20.15)36/2,598,960

20.16)26,334/2,598,960   20.17)3003/2,598,960   20.18)1287/65,780   20.19)6/65,780   20.20)45/1287

20.21)1287/575,757   20.22)65,780/575,757   20.23)21,420/575,757   20.24)12,650/65,780   20.25)3876/65,780

20.26)2600/98,280   20.27)1456/98,280

Group 21: 21.1)2,598,960   21.2)a)4 b)0.00000153   21.3)a)ace through 9 b)36 c)0.00001385   21.4)a)13 b)48 c)624 d)0.0002401   21.5)c)48 d)78 e)3744 f)0.001441   21.6)a)5148 b)5108 c)0.001965   21.7)a)40 b)256 c)10240 d)10,200 e)0.003925   21.8)a)54,912 b)0.02113   21.9)a)123,552 b)0.04754   21.10)a)1,098,240 b)0.4226   21.11)a)1,302,540 b)0.5012   21.12)a)575,757   b)3/575,757   c)27/575,757   d)468/575,757 e)3861/575,757 f)2430/575,757 g)7722/575,757 h)23,166/575,757 i)231,660/575,757

Group 22:   22.1)a)48 b)9,10,J,Q,K,A c)12 d)8 e)24   22.2)a)1,712,304   22.3)a)32 b)128 b)0.00007475 22.4)a)128 b)0.00007475   22.5)a)336 b)0.0001962   22.6)a)16,800 b)0.009811   22.7)a)3168 b)2912 c)480;0.0002803 d)1920;0.001121 e)512;0.000299   22.8)a)47,040 b)0.02747   22.9)a)16 b)4096 c)65,536 d)65,280 e)0.03812   22.10)a)215,040 b)0.1256   22.11)a)375,840 b)0.2195   22.12)a)858,240 b)0.5021   22.13)a)130,560 b)0.07625   22.16)a)376,992 b)96/376,992 c)96/376,992 d)36/376,992 e)2700/376,992 f)9000/376,992 g)360/376,992 h)1440/376,992 i) 43,200/376,992   22.17)a)658,008 b)128/658,008 c)11,200/658,008 d)240/658,008 e)640/658,008 f)32,768/658,008

Group 23: 23.1)a)82,160 b)prob: 0.014, 0.139, 0.847 c)1/6.55 = 0.153 = 0.014+0.0139   23.2)i)4 spot 1/3.86=0.259 ii)2 spot 1/16.63=0.060   23.3)a)80 b)prob:0.25, 0.75 c)1/4 = 0.25   23.4)a)3160 b)prob:0.06, 0.94 c)1/16.63 = 0.06 23.5)a)n b)w c)l=n−w d)a e)nCa f)(wCa)/(nCa) g)(wC0)(lCa)/(nCa) h)1−answer from g) i)(wC2)(lC(a− 2))/(nCa) 23.6)a)292,201,338   b)1/292,201,338   c)25/292,201,338   d)20,160/292,201,338   e)280,450,800/292,201,338 f)1/24.87=0.0402=1−0.9598   23.7)a)19,600 b)prob:0.006, 0.092, 0.902 c)0.098   23.8)a)12,103,014 b)3003/12,103,014 c)675,675/12,103,014   23.9)a)1,581,580   b)prob:0.003, 0.043, 0.213, 0.741   c)0.259   23.10)a)23,535,820 b)45/23,535,820 c)6,375,600/23,535,820 d)1,081,575/23,535,820

Group 24: 24.1)a)lose $0.50 b)lose $0.34 c)$0.50 d)$0.66 e)no, expect to lose   24.2)a)$0.55 b)yes, expect to win c)$1.55   24.3)a)12,271,512 b)# of ways in table (and product): 1 (0.081); 252 (0.021); 12,915 (0.042); 229,600 (0.056); 1,678,950 (0.137); 10,349,794 (0); expectation: lose $0.66   c)lose $2409   d)$1241   e)$3650   f)jar!   24.4)lose $0.83 24.5)a)$0 b)$1; it is fair   24.6)a)lose $0.32 b)lose $1.60 c)$0.18

Group 25: 25.1)a)1/38 b)$35 c)lose 5¢   25.2)a)36/38 b)$17 c)lose 5¢   25.3)$0   25.4)a)34 to 4 b)$1 c)lose 5¢ 25.5)$0   25.6)a)5/38 b)$6 c)lose 8¢   25.7)lose 5¢   25.8)lose 5¢   25.9)a)18/38 b)$1 c)lose 5¢   25.10)true; to make $ 25.11)5 #'s; $0.08; $8.00   25.12) a) lose $0.17, b) no   25.13)$15   25.14)$4.11   25.15)win $0.65, so yes 25.16)a)lose $0.19, so no   25.17)a)lose $4.28 b)$0.72   25.18)$0 so it's fair

Group 26: 26.1)a)2652 b)16/51 c)4/51   26.2)a)1326 b)64 c)0.0483   26.3)b)i)0.0478 ii)0.0476 iii)0.0475 26.4)a)-1 b)6 c)T=1.2; minimum bet (base amount) d)T=3; bet 2 times your base amount   26.5)a)134,940 b)0.0474 26.6)a)2/38 b)36/38 c)2 to 36 d)$1700 e))lose $0.05

151

TEST 2 REVIEW: 1)a)1/6 b)5/6 c)5/6 d)1/6 e)switch 2)a)66/1326 b)66 to 1260 3) 4:48 4) 16 to 36
5) 1/7 6)a)40/250 b)130/250 c)110/250 d)90/250 e)70/110 f)70/160 g)160/200 h)40/90 i)50/140 7)6/36
8)a)4/36 b)6/36 c)30/36 d)8/36 e)1/5 f)2/4 9)a)i)5/38 ii)33/38 b)i)33 to 5 ii)5 to 33 c)$60 d)lose $.08
10)a)1/1000 b)243/1000 c)432/1000 11)a)1/64 b)6/64 c)20/64 d)63/64 12)a)210/715 b)55/715 c)165/715
d)145/715 13) 7/26 14)a)36/91 b)55/91 c)28/91 d)63/91 15)a)4998/5005 b)175/5005 16)a)712,842/2,598,960
b)56/2,598,960 c)658,008/2,598,960 d)4560/2,598,960 17)225/455 18)a)win $1.66 b)yes, expect to win 19)a)−66¢
b)34¢ 20)a)6,5;2/6 b)3,2,1;3/6 c)4;1/6 21) a)43,680/1,712,304 b)8436/1,712,304 c)224/201,376 22)0.0000001609
23)a)54,740 b)5775/54,740 c)28,505/54,740 24)a)45/8,259,888 b)3,575,000/8,259,888 25)a)P(has| test +) b)0.6346
26)a)33,670 b)1600/33,670

OPTIONAL GROUP: 2)a)16 b)i)TTTT ii)TTTH, TTHT, THTT, HTTT iii)TTHH, THTH, THHT, HTTH, HTHT,
HHTT iv)THHH, HTHH, HHTH, HHHT v)HHHH c)i)0.0625 ii)0.25 iii)0.375 iv)0.25 v)0.0625 4)1.5 5)0−6;
16 b)0/0, 0/1, 1/0, 1/1, 2/0, 0/2, 1/2, 2/1, 0/3, 3/0, 2/2, 1/3, 3/1, 3/2, 2/3, 3/3 c)i)1/16 ii)2/16 iii)3/16 iv)4/16 v)3/16
vi)2/16 vii)1/16 d)3 e)i)0 ii)0 iii)1/4 iv)1/4 v)1/4 vi)1/4 vii)0 viii)no, just not 0, 1, or 6 6)a)0−9; 64 b)i)0/0/0
ii)0/0/1, 0/1/0, 1/0/0 iii)0/0/2, 0/2/0, 2/0/0, 0/1/1, 1/0/1, 1/1/0 iv)0/0/3, 0/3/0, 3/0/0, 0/1/2, 0/2/1, 1/0/2, 1/2/0, 2/0/1, 2/1/0,
1/1/1 v)0/1/3, 0/3/1, 1/0/3, 1/3/0, 3/0/1, 3/1/0, 0/2/2, 2/0/2, 2/2/0, 1/1/2, 1/2/1, 2/1/1 c)i)1/64 ii)3/64 iii)6/64 iv)10/64
v)12/64 vi)12/64 vii)10/64 viii)6/64 ix)3/64 x)1/64 d)4 or 5 e)i)3 ii)4 iii)5 iv)6 f)4 because you could guess that
they have 0 coins and the other could have ~1.5 7)a)2048 b)165/2048 c)1/2048 d)67/2048 e)2047/2048 8)a)0.1123
b)0.5201 c)essentially 1

3	4	5	2	1	6
6	2	1	5	4	3
4	5	6	1	3	2
2	1	3	4	6	5
1	3	2	6	5	4
5	6	4	3	2	1

FINAL EXAM REVIEW

1)

Jessica	Maggie	Annie	Lily	Naomi
Trotter	Bore	Hazlitt	Piggott	Sowter
sausage	pie	ham	chops	Scotch eggs

2)943 3)

4)23 5)a)T b)F c)T d)U e){f,h,i,k,l,m,n,o,p} f){ } g)7 h){e,f,g,h,j} i){e,g,j,k,l,p} j){},{k},{l},{p},{k,l},
{k,p},{l,p},{k,l,p} k)128 6)$B^c \cap A$ 7){1,9} 8)a)i)nothing in A, nothing in C, but everything else ii)those who
don't eat apples or cantaloupe b)i)only the two sections of C that are not in B ii)those who eat cantaloupe but not bananas
9)21 10) 1/11 11)a)170 b)80 c)120 d)15 12)1,404,000 13)45 14)3024 15)924 16)384 17)5to8
18)37/256 19)a)1/52 b)16/52 c)28/52 d)4/40 e)3/39 20) AA, BB, ABA, BAB, ABB, BAA 21)a)0 b)3/6 c)3/6
22)a)778,320/2,598,960 b)2,023,203/2,598,960 c)123,552/2,598,960 23)a)731,120/1,712,304 b)1,335,312/1,712,304
c)376,320/1,712,304 24)10/50 25)a)6/36 b)2/6 26)95/1001 27)a)4/38 b)34 to 4 c)lose $0.05 d)$80 28)a)win
$2.50 b)yes, expect to win $ 29)2596/3276 30)a)30/455 b)60/2730 31)a)P(has|+) b)0.8181 32)a)lose $0.85
b)$1.15 33)a)142,506 b)252/142,506 c)22,800/142,506 34) 3136/66,066 35)a)100,000 b)59,049/100,000
c)810/100,000 d)40,951/100,000 36)switch because P(car if you switch)= 11/12 and P(car if you stay)=1/12

REFERENCES

Aufmann, Richard N., Lockwood, Joanne S., Nation, Richard D., and Clegg, Daniel K., *Mathematical Excursions*, 2nd ed., Houghton Mifflin Company, 2007.

Brase, Charles Henry and Brase, Corrinne Pellillo, *Understandable Statistics: Concepts and Methods*, 8th ed., Houghton Mifflin Company, 2006.

Burger, Edward B. and Starbird, Michael, *The Heart of Mathematics: An invitation to effective thinking*, Key College Publishing, 2005.

For All Practical Purposes: Mathematics Literacy In Today's World, 7th ed., W. H. Freeman and Company, New York, 2006.

Grochowski, John, *The Casino Answer Book*, Bonus Books, Inc., 1998.

Grochowski, John, *The Slot Machine Answer Book*, 2nd ed., Bonus Books, Inc., 2005.

Haigh, John, *Taking Chances: Winning with Probability*, Oxford University Press, 2003.

Johnson, David B. and Mowry, Thomas A., *Mathematics: A Practical Odyssey*, 6th ed., Thomas Learning, Inc., 2007.

Nolan, Joseph and Jacqueline Wroughton, "Pinochle Poker: An Activity For Counting and Probability", *Journal of Statistics Education*, Volume 20, Number 2, 2012, from www.amstat.org/publications/jse/v20n2/wroughton.pdf

Packel, Edward, *The Mathematics of Games and Gambling*, 2nd ed., The Mathematical Association of America, 2006.

The Way to Play: the Illustrated Encyclopedia of the Games of the World, Bantam Books, 1975.

Zaslavsky, Claudia, *Africa Counts: Number and Pattern in African Culture*, 3rd ed., Lawrence Hill Books, Chicago, 1999.

Zaslavsky, Claudia, *The Multicultural Classroom: Bringing in the World*, Heinemann, Portsmouth, NH, 1996.

Websites:

https://www.blackjackinfo.com/no-6-to-5-blackjack/

http://www.braingle.com/Logic-Grid.html

http://education.ti.com/go/NUMB3RS

www.powerball.com

http://worldspoofers.com/